Alexander Geddes

Prospectus of a New Translation of the Holy Bible

From Corrected Texts of the originals, compared with ancient versions - with various readings, explanatory notes, and critical observations

Alexander Geddes

Prospectus of a New Translation of the Holy Bible
From Corrected Texts of the originals, compared with ancient versions - with various readings, explanatory notes, and critical observations

ISBN/EAN: 9783337170462

Printed in Europe, USA, Canada, Australia, Japan

Cover: Foto ©Lupo / pixelio.de

More available books at **www.hansebooks.com**

PROSPECTUS

OF A

NEW TRANSLATION

OF THE

HOLY BIBLE

FROM CORRECTED TEXTS OF THE ORIGINALS, COMPARED
WITH THE ANCIENT VERSIONS.

WITH

VARIOUS READINGS, EXPLANATORY NOTES, AND
CRITICAL OBSERVATIONS.

BY

The Rev. ALEXANDER GEDDES, L.L.D.

GLASGOW:

PRINTED FOR THE AUTHOR, AND SOLD BY R. FAULDER, BOND STREET,
LONDON; C. ELIOT, EDINBURGH; AND —— CROSS, DUBLIN.
M.DCC.LXXXVI.

TO THE RIGHT HONOURABLE

LORD PETRE.

P ERMIT me, My Lord, to prefent you with the firft fruits of many years painful labour; in the pleafing hope of being, one day, able to lay before you the whole harveft. That *thefe* or *that* will be worthy of your Lordship's and the Public's acceptance, it would be prefumptuous in me to fay, but is extremely natural for me to wifh. Meanwhile, I have the honour to be, with very great refpect,

    My Lord,

        Your Lordfhip's

            Ever grateful and

                Moft obedient humble fervant,

                      A. G.

TO THE READER.

THE following Prospectus was fairly written out for the press nearly two years ago. This, it is hoped, will account for some things being added in the notes, which, perhaps, might have been more properly incorporated in the text. In reading over the printed sheets, I have observed some typographical errors, the principal of which are corrected on the reverse of this leaf: but there is a mistake page 100 line 15, that needs to be apologized for. An edition of the New Testament is there said to have been mentioned before, although it is not mentioned till afterwards, in the note, p. 131, which the reader is requested to attend to.

TYPOGRAPHICAL ERRORS.

Page 32. in the note read—*Septuaginta*.
    36. in the note read—counsils.
    38. l. 10. read—a more correct.
    63. l. 11. read—persuade.
    110. l. 5. read—translators.
    116. l. 9. read—Oecumenius.
    121. l. 5. read—*memoires*.
    137. l. 19. read—exclude.
    8. 9. *pertinacity*

PROSPECTUS

OF A

NEW TRANSLATION

OF THE

HOLY BIBLE.

HAVING long made the HOLY SCRIPTURES and the languages in which they were originally written, my particular study, I ventured, some years ago, to give an *Idea* of a new Translation of the whole BIBLE; at the request of a person of distinction, who wished I would undertake such a work. That sketch, imperfect as it was, meeting with the approbation of some of the most learned and respectable characters in the kingdom, I have been since advised by my friends to publish a more ample *Prospectus;* and, for many reasons, I find myself strongly disposed to follow their advice.

For although it must be yet some considerable time, before the Translation itself will be ready for the press, there can be no impropriety in letting the learned public know, that it is preparing; and putting it in the power of those who choose it, to help me with their counsel and assistance, in the prosecution of so laborious and arduous an undertaking.

That a new Translation of the Bible, particularly of the Old Testament, is still wanted, I shall assume as a position generally agreed upon. To explore the causes that have concurred to render former Translations defective, and to point out the means and method by which a part of their defects may be removed, is the intention of this PROSPECTUS; which I now deliver to the public, with all that anxious diffidence, which the great importance of the subject and the mediocrity of my abilities demand.

The first and principal cause of the imperfection of almost all modern Translations of the Bible is to be sought for in the imperfection and incorrectness of the originals, from which they were made; for, when the text to be translated is itself corrupted, the translation must necessarily participate of its corruption: but modern translations of the Bible have, almost all, been made from a text in many places corrupted: How then could they fail to be, at least, equally faulty?

It is an assertion no less strange than true, that the text of scarcely any profane author of note has been so incorrectly published as that of the Hebrew Scriptures. To restore Demosthenes, Tully, Virgil, Horace, as nearly as possible, to their first integrity, no human pains have been spared: libraries have been ransacked, manuscripts collated, parallel places compared, history, geography, criticism alternately called in to assistance: and happy was the man who, after a length of time, and with immense labour, could fill up the smallest chasm; detect the most insignificant interpolation; rectify a single transposition; alter a single sentence, or change a single letter to the improvement of his favourite author. This sort of labour gave celebrity, during the two last centuries, to many persons of real genius and learning; and although, in these days of pretended refinement and philosophy, we are too apt to call them pedants, and to depretiate their studies; yet to them we certainly owe a great part of the pleasure which we find in perusing the works of antiquity.

But why were not the same pains taken, and the same means employed, to give a correct edition of the Bible? and how is it, that, of all edited books, it still remains the most incorrect that ever came from the press? Was it accounted of less importance than the rest? Not so: both Jews and Christians, the orthodox and the separatist, equally considered it as the richest treasure they could possess; as a code of laws and a system of morality delivered to them from Heaven; the object of their belief and the rule of their conduct; in short, the Book of books; compared with which, all other compositions are trifling and vain.

Were the editors, then, ignorant or careless? Quite the contrary: many of them were men of uncommon erudition; and all of them boasted of the incredible pains they had been at, to give to their several editions, as great a degree of perfection, as can be attained by human industry. This was their uniform language, from Bomberg to Vanderhooght; and it must be allowed that, in some respects, their diligence was, at least, equal to their learning.

Had they exerted the same talents, and taken the same pains to correct the text, by such helps as yet remained; as they employed to preserve and embellish it, in its state of depravation; we might have, long since, been in the possession of a copy of the Hebrew Scriptures, as nearly perfect as, at this distance of time, we can reasonably look for; and freed, at least, from innumerable imperfections that still disgrace it: but the more those men laboured, the less they may be said to have advanced; and we scruple not to affirm that the celebrated edition of Amsterdam in 1705, is a less valuable copy of the primitive Hebrew text, than that which was printed at Soncino, nearly 300 years ago*.

It could not, indeed, well be otherwise. The editors, or at least the correctors of the press, were generally Jews; entirely devoted to their rabbinical prejudices. By these they appretiated the manuscript that was to serve as an archetype for the impression. The Masora was to those text-torturers the bed of Procrustes, to the exact length and breadth of which every word was to be fitted with the greatest precision; and, this pretended standard being once established as infallible, all posterior editions were judged to be accurate

* In 1489. See Fabricy *Titres Primitifs*.

or erroneous, only as far as they agreed or disagreed with it.

To some it may seem hard to conceive, how the learned of the Christian persuasion should have adopted the same ideas; and, in this point, given implicit credit to a set of men, whom, in almost every other respect, they believed to be the vilest impostors. Several causes, however, concurred to beget and propagate this gross delusion.

The study of Hebrew, which had been but little cultivated among Christians, even in the brightest periods of Christianity, had now for many ages been almost totally neglected. The first teachers of it, on the revival of letters, were Jews, or converts from Judaism. These failed not to impress upon the minds of their too credulous disciples the highest ideas of the learning of the Masoretes, and of their scrupulous attention to preserve the sacred records from every shadow of error, by means of a certain canon of divine origin, traditionally handed down to them from their great law-giver Moses; or, at least, from the prophet Ezra. Independent of this canon the scriptures were, they affirmed, a locked-up treasure. The Masora was both a key to open, and a hedge to guard them: the very grammar of the language in which they were written could not be learned without it.

The scholars of those pedagogues became pedagogues in their turn; and as we are ever apt to think that method of attaining science the best, which we have followed, especially if it has been a painful one, they inculcated to their pupils the absolute necessity of purſuing the ſame rugged and thorny path, which they had themſelves purſued before, as the only one that could lead, directly and infallibly, to the ſanctuary of holy writ. Thus, with the firſt elements of Hebrew learning, were propagated in the Chriſtian ſchools the moſt ridiculous notions of the Rabbins; and no one called in queſtion their bold aſſertions, becauſe no one ſuppoſed he could know any thing of the matter, but through them *.

Beſides, it was a flattering conſideration to thoſe who believed the Bible to be from God, to think that God had provided for it a perpetual ſafeguard, which ſhould ſecure every word, ſyllable, letter, and apex from all ſorts of corruption or alteration, to the end of time. They did not think of enquiring how this ſame ſecurity had, for ſo many ages, been itſelf ſecured; nor did they reflect, that, if it had ever been the intention of the Deity to preſerve, in a miraculous manner, the primitive text of ſcripture from ſuch accidental errors, as all other writings are liable to, it would have been more agreeable to what we know of his wiſdom, to have made the miracle accompany the text itſelf, than, leaving the text to common riſks, have provided a ſeparate oral canon, by which it

---

* Hence it ſoon became a ſort of axiom among theologians, that a thorough knowledge of the Hebrew could not be acquired without the aid of the Maſora; and that none but a ſkilful Maſorete could give a good edition of the Bible. Theſe prepoſſeſſions were ſo deeply rooted, that they kept their ground for almoſt three centuries, and are not yet quite eradicated. They were adopted, in part, even by F. Simon; in other reſpects, a critic of great acumen, and no way a ſlave to inveterate opinions.

might, from time to time, be rectified, and which should have the wonderful privilege of being liable to no corruption; a canon, too, so prolix, so intricate, and so confused as the Masora *.

Nor did they call to mind, that those of the first Christians who had studied the Hebrew, while it was yet, in some measure, a living tongue, were totally ignorant of such a canon; and knew of no other rules for correcting the scriptures, but a careful collation of the best manuscripts, and the use of a sober criticism. They overlooked even the obvious argument which they might have drawn from a comparison of the New Testament, their own peculiar code, with the Old, which more particularly appertained to the Jews. For the former, they could not be ignorant, God had provided no such security; why should he have done it for the latter? giving more to the figure than to the reality, and preferring the son of the bond woman to that of the free? To these, and other absurdities, connected with this opinion, they did not attend: it was enough for them that it flattered their prejudices and favoured their belief: that alone was sufficient to give it a general currency.

It is not, however, probable that so base a metal could have long continued to circulate, if it had not received a new degree of

---

* The English reader, who wishes to have some idea of the Masora, may consult *Simon's critical history of the Old Testament, Prideaux's connections,* or *Kennicott's second dissertation on the state of the Hebrew text.*

credit from the revolution in religion that happened soon after. The Proteſtants, on ſeparating from the communion of Rome, ſeem to have thought they could not get at too great a diſtance*. Finding it convenient to appeal from the deciſions of a living aſſembly to the dead letter of ſcripture, they conſidered themſelves as under a neceſſity of maintaining, that the ſcripture-text was not only incorrupted, but even incorruptible; and as the Maſoretic ſyſtem favoured this hypotheſis, they adopted it without heſitation, and defended it with more pertinacy than even the Jews themſelves. To recede from it in the ſmalleſt degree, was, they imagined, to open a door for Popery, by overturning this fundamental article of Proteſtantiſm, "That the ſcripture alone is a ſufficient and infal-"lible rule of faith."

So generally diffuſed, and ſo ſtrongly rivetted was this prejudice, that when Capellus firſt ventured to unclinch it, in his *Critica Sacra*, he was accounted a ſort of apoſtate from the ſound doctrine of the reformed churches, and could not find a Proteſtant bookſeller to print his work. And, what is ſtill more ſtrange, when

---

* Many other inſtances could be given of this diſpoſition to run into extremes. "Some of "our reformed brethren" (ſays Biſhop Berkley in the character of Crito) "becauſe the Ro-"maniſts attributed too much to the fathers, ſeem to have attributed too little to them, from "a very uſual, though no very judicious oppoſition." Min. Phil. Dial. vi. Sect. 27.—Reynolds thought it a ſufficient reaſon to reject altogether the uſe of the croſs, becauſe the Papiſts had *abuſed* it; and ſome of the Scotch Calviniſts had ſuch averſion to liturgies and ſet forms of prayer, that they would not uſe even that of our Lord.

Dr. Kennicott, not many years ago, published his excellent *Dissertations* on the state of the Hebrew text, those were not wanting, even in this country, who brought the same charges against him as had been formerly brought against Capellus; nor did it depend on them, that the greatest literary undertaking of this, or indeed of any other age, was not quashed in its very beginning, as hurtful to Christianity.

It cannot be denied, that the Catholic divines in general formed a sounder judgment of the state of the Hebrew text than the generality of Protestants. Whether it was always a sincere love for the truth, or sometimes an excessive partiality for the Vulgate version, that made them so keen and clear-sighted in discovering the faults of the original, I will not take upon me to determine: but the fact is certain, they generally judged rightly of the then state of the original; and there are few passages of it impugned as erroneous by Bellarmine, Gordon*, Morinus, &c. which are not now acknowledged to be so by the most learned Protestants.

From this, however, it is true some Catholic writers drew conclusions, that were by no means fairly deducible. They argued,

---

* James Gordon (commonly called *Huntlaeus*, because of the Huntly family, to distinguish him from another Jesuit of the same name of the family of Lesmore) was one of the most acute and artful adversaries of the present Hebrew text. It was to oppose his little tract *De Verbo Dei*, that Glassius wrote his *Philologia Sacra*. Gordon's stile is clear and concise; and his arguments generally conclusive. It must be confessed, however, that he extols the Vulgate above measure, and advances some unsupportable propositions.

that, becaufe the Hebrew text was in many places corrupted, where the Vulgate was not; therefore the Vulgate was, every where, preferable to the Hebrew text. The ftrange mifconception of a decree of the Council of Trent gave rife, or at leaft new ftrength to this abfurd opinion. That Synod had declared the Vulgate to be an authentic verfion of the Scripture, in the plain and obvious fenfe we fhall fee in the fequel; yet the word *authentic* became a fubject of eager controverfy in the Catholic univerfities: fome affirming it only meant, that the Vulgate was in general a faithful verfion, containing nothing contrary to faith or morality, and having every thing neceffary to conftitute an authentic document; while others contended, with more zeal than prudence, that it implied an abfolute and exclufive authenticity in the ftricteft fenfe of the word; which gave it a preference and fuperiority not only over all other tranflations, but alfo over the originals themfelves. It is to be remarked that this laft opinion was that of the moft ignorant, the former that of the moft learned of the Catholic theologians; and that they, who were the foremoft in depreffing the Hebrew text to enhance the value of the Vulgate, were the leaft of all qualified to appretiate the merits of either. At prefent there feems to be but one opinion on this fubject; and that is, luckily, the right one.

With regard to the ftate of the Hebrew text, there has of late been a wonderful revolution in the minds of men. Proteftants and

Catholics seem to have changed sides; and while many of the former, in every country, find *errata* in it by thousands, there are some of the latter, who can hardly discern in it any error at all. Thus it is, and thus it always will be, where parties are concerned. What is particularly relished by one, will, for that very reason, be disliked by another; and few, very few indeed, will be found, on either side, to hold that golden medium, beyond which the truth is vainly sought for. Here the truth is, at least so to me it appears, that the original Hebrew text is neither so very much corrupted as some Catholics of former, and many Protestants of latter days affirm, nor yet so void of errors as some Catholics of this, and almost all the Protestants of the last age maintained it to be. Still, however, its most strenuous advocates, whether Catholic or Protestant, will now, we presume, be obliged to confess, that it is evidently more or less erroneous*; and, consequently, that it is the

---

* The sticklers for the absolute integrity of the Hebrew text have so often changed their ground, and assumed so many different positions, that it requires, if not great skill, at least much patience to continue the contest with them. Their first grand palladium was the Masora, under the protection of which they deemed their fortress impregnable. Capellus did not, like Ulysses, rob them of their sacred guardian; he stormed their citadel in despite of her, and revealed to the wondering world her impotency to defend them.—Forced from this hold, they took possession of another. " Let it be granted," said they, " that the Masora is of rab-
" binical, not divine authority; yet the wonderful uniformity of all the Hebrew manu-
" scripts, and their perfect agreement with the printed copy is the strongest evidence of the
" integrity of the latter; and implies, if not a miraculous preservation of the text, an atten-
" tion in the copyists that borders on a miracle." This was long a capital and a favourite argument. It was an argument founded on a matter of fact, which even Capellus did not

PROSPECTUS.

firſt duty of a tranſlator to examine into, and aſcertain its errors; to trace them up, if poſſible, to their ſource; and endeavour to remove them by every mean in his power.

chuſe to deny; becauſe it was aſſerted with ſuch confidence, and becauſe he had no direct proofs of the contrary. In vain he attacked them with other weapons; in vain he proved that the ancients had frequently read otherwiſe than we do; in vain he ſhewed that the preſent reading is often improbable, ſometimes ſeemingly abſurd: ſtill the pretended uniformity of all the copies was conſidered as an unſurmountable obſtacle, even by many of thoſe who, in other reſpects, acknowledged the full force of Capellus's reaſoning; and, thus, his opponents inſultingly triumphed, under the ſecurity of a mere preſumption. When, by an actual examination and collation of manuſcripts, they were at length driven out of this poſt alſo, they ſought ſecurity for themſelves, by trying to make their adverſaries invidious; and held forth to the public the dreadful conſequences to religion, if it ſhould be once allowed that the Scriptures had not come down to us in their full original purity. In this new mode of warfare, they employed ſtratagems not much to their honour. They imputed to the defenders of the oppoſite ſyſtem, views which they never dreamed of, and ſentiments which they openly diſavowed. The advantage that aroſe from ſuch diſingenuous artifices, could not be of long duration. The diſcerning public ſoon perceived the weakneſs of an argument merely negative, oppoſed to facts and demonſtrations; and the popular odium, which its abettors had endeavoured to throw on others, was turned into a ſtream of ridicule againſt themſelves. They now ſeem diſpoſed to give up the divine authority of the Maſora, the miraculous preſervation of the text, and even its abſolute integrity through any means whatever: but ſtill they ſtrenuouſly defend the abſolute ſuperiority of the preſent printed copy, to all other copies or verſions; and maintain, that we have no right to alter or correct it, even on the authority of manuſcripts. Hear their reaſon. "The firſt editors of the Hebrew Bible had manu-
" ſcripts as well as we, and probably more ancient and correct manuſcripts than now exiſt: the
" new critic-collators have not yet found one ſo correct, in the whole, as the printed copy;
" therefore, the printed copy is not to be corrected by manuſcripts confeſſedly more errone-
" ous than itſelf." Never was the abuſe of logic carried to a greater exceſs. We will grant, what perhaps we ſhould not grant, that the preſent printed text is, in the whole, more correct than any ſingle manuſcript: does it hence follow, that, in every particular part, it is more correct than all the manuſcripts together; or even than ſome one individual manuſcript, ſingly conſidered? Had the firſt editors accurately deſcribed the manuſcripts they uſed, and

All the corruptions, that get into the text of any writing, are owing either to defign or overfight. Whether or not any parts of the Hebrew fcriptures have been defignedly corrupted, is a queftion, that was early agitated in the Chriftian church; and, for the firft four centuries, the affirmative feems to have been the prevailing opinion, among both the Greek and Latin fathers. That opinion, which the authority of Saint Jerom * and Saint Auguftine had, in a great meafure, rendered obfolete for many ages, has, in modern times, been revived and warmly defended by critics of the firft abilities, and as warmly oppofed by others of equal celebrity.

indicated the repofitories they were to be found in; we fhould have it in our power to compare them with the printed text, and with one another, and be able to form a better judgment, both of the fidelity of the editors, and of the refpective merit of their manufcripts; or, if thefe no more exifted, we fhould know, at leaft, that they are loft. As things are, the faireft inference we can draw, and the moft favourable judgment we can form is this, that the editors followed the beft manufcripts they could find. But fo did all other firft editors, if they were not fools: yet it has never, I think, been affirmed that pofterior editions, of any other book but the Bible, might not, and may not ftill, be improved by a collation of more manufcripts; fhould thefe even, taken feparately, be lefs correct and valuable than the firft that were ufed. But what if I fhould affert that there are feveral fingle manufcripts of the Hebrew fcriptures; any one of which is a more correct copy of the original, than the printed one? what method would they take to redargue my affertion; and by what criterion could the queftion between us be rationally decided? By none other, I prefume, than analogy and circumftantial evidence, examined at the bar of found and fober criticifm.

* This father is not always confiftent with himfelf. Sometimes he pofitively charges the Jews with having wilfully corrupted the text; at other times, he feems to exculpate them of this grievous accufation. We will not fay, with Simon, that when he accufes them he fpeaks againft his own fentiments; but rather fuppofe, that he afterwards changed them, as many other honeft men have done.

PROSPECTUS.

There is this observable difference, however, in their respective modes of reasoning. The former support their sentiment by positive arguments and indisputable facts; whereas the latter ground theirs, chiefly, on negative improbabilities, and the dangerous consequences which flow, they pretend, from the opposite hypothesis. I shall have occasion, elsewhere, to treat largely on this subject: at present I shall only say that the truth still appears to be in the middle. For although we should not, perhaps, easily admit that so many passages have been designedly corrupted, as a certain class of writers would have us believe; yet it cannot, I think, be well denied, that there are, in some instances, such strong marks of wilful contamination, as to leave little room for doubt.

But by far the greater part of Biblical corruptions, are to be ascribed to the same ordinary causes, that produce them in all other writings; the ignorance, the carelessness, the inaccuracy of copyists; and as the number of such corruptions, in any writing, is generally in proportion to the number of years it has existed, and the number of times it has been copied; is it to be wondered that the Hebrew text of the Bible should, at this day, contain a very great number of such corruptions? It would be a wonder indeed, if it did not: for how could it be, with any shew of reason, imagined, that a book so old as the Bible; written in a language, that has long since ceased to be vernacular; transcribed by so many different persons, in so many different places; and under so many different circumstances and situations; through all that vicissitude of fortune, that has attended the Jewish people; should have contracted no spot nor blemish, in the course of two thousand years? That waters, which have rolled for ages through a thousand different soils and channels, should be still as pure and untainted as when they issued from their primitive source, would be far less wonderful, than that the Hebrew scriptures should have remained in their first integrity.

Beside these circumstantial and extraneous causes of mistake, that are more or less common to them with all old writings, there are others which make the Hebrew scriptures particularly liable to chirographical errors; and which may be called intrinsic sources of corruption. At one period, the whole text was changed from the Hebrew to the Chaldee characters*. Many of the letters in both alphabets have a strong resemblance to one another; and, in, some of them, the diacritic marks are hardly distinguishable. The invention of vowel-points, by rendering the genuine vocal elements quiescent, gave frequently occasion to throw them out as useless; and that very thing, which was absurdly looked upon as the chief preservative of the sacred text from future errors, largely contributed to make it still more erroneous.

If, with all this, we take into consideration the colloquial tauto-

* This at least is the common belief; and the arguments that have been urged against it, appear not sufficient to overturn it.

logy of the Scripture ſtile, the frequent occurrence of the ſame words and phraſes, the repetition of the ſame or nearly the ſame ſentences, the proximity and contiguity of the ſame terminations, the conſtant return of the ſame particles, pronouns and proper names, and the deceptions continually ariſing from the aſſociation of ideas, ſimilarity of ſounds and equivalence of meaning, we ſhall be obliged to confeſs that it was ſcarcely poſſible for the moſt diligent and attentive tranſcriber to avoid committing many overſights.

That many ſuch overſights have been actually committed, and that a great number of corruptions have, by that means, gradually crept into the text, are poſitions which have, of late, been ſo invincibly eſtabliſhed, that no one, we truſt, will in future preſume to call them in queſtion. But let not this alarm the pious reader, as if the authenticity of the Scriptures were thereby weakened, or their authority rendered precarious. Were it neceſſary, to conſtitute an authentic deed, that the moſt recent and remote copies of it ſhould be exactly the ſame with the firſt autograph, there would be no ſuch thing in the world as any ancient authentic deed, of which the autograph had been loſt: there could be no ſuch thing, without a continual miracle. It is enough, that there is ſufficient evidence of its being eſſentially the ſame with the original; and that the changes it has undergone, whether from deſign or accident, are not ſuch as can affect its authority, as a genuine record.

Such, preciſely, is the caſe of the Hebrew ſcriptures. Notwithstanding all the various corruptions of whatsoever sort, that now disfigure them; it is as certain, as any position of this kind can possibly be, that they are still essentially the same; and that the whole historical tenor of the divine oeconomy towards man has been preserved in them, without any important alteration, to the present time. Take the most modern and most imperfect transcript of their originals, that now exists; or even the most erroneous copy of the most erroneous version, that ever was made from them; and you shall find in it every thing that is absolutely necessary to constitute an authentic writing; and to answer all the great purposes, for which they were intended *.

* From this acknowledgement, made by all those who have been the foremost to detect the corruptions of the Hebrew text, some persons have drawn this ridiculous conclusion; That it is therefore unnecessary, nay unexpedient, to correct it at all. Since it is allowed, say they, to be still essentially the same, and to contain every thing necessary to salvation, what need is there to trouble the peace of the world with collations, amendments, &c? The a- nonymous French author of a series of petulant and declamatory letters, addressed to Dr. Kennicott, urges this argument in the following extraordinary manner: " If the great ar- " ticles of the Christian faith are untouched in the text which we already have, why disturb " the church with corrections and innovations that are of no service to religion? What ad- " vantage will accrue to Christians from knowing, that *Jacob* is written sometimes with a *vau* " and sometimes without a *vau?* Or that in the word *David* there was no *jod* before the Ba- " bylonish captivity? Is the incarnation of Jesus Christ the less true for that, &c." No; nor would it be less true, if the entire book of Job or the Song of Solomon were wanting. The chain of religion would be uninterrupted without either, yet we should be exceedingly sorry they were lost. We can make a shift to do without the original text of Ecclesiasticus; al- though it is devoutly to be wished that it still existed. There were once many pieces of He- brew scripture, of which we have not now even a translation: will it be said that, because the incarnation of Christ can be ascertained without their aid, it would be of no utility to

C

For beside the internal marks of genuineness, which they super-eminently possess; they are supported by such a continued and closely connected chain of external evidence, as is not to be met with in favour of any other composition whatever. Who, but the paradoxical Hardouin, ever doubted of the authenticity of Plato's dialogues, or Demosthenes's orations? yet they have come down to us with not half the number of vouchers, that accompany the Jewish writings; and it would be easier to find ingenious arguments to prove that *those* were invented by the monks in the thirteenth century, than that *these* were fabricated at any particular period.

It is true they have been transmitted with many errors, and are at this day extremely incorrect: but, here again, they have an advantage over most other writings; the means of correcting them are more obvious and abundant. What these are, and how they are to be employed, it is now time to enquire.

The first source of emendation of any writing is the collation and comparison of manuscripts; a source but recently opened with respect to the Hebrew scriptures; and not yet so deeply explored, as we hope it will soon be.

---

religion, that they could still be recovered? Every thing must be of utility to religion that tends to corroborate the great charters on which it is grounded, or to restore them to their original purity, were it but the addition or retrenchment of a single letter. For the rest, there are few of the amendments proposed to be made in the Hebrew text from the collation of manuscripts, of so very little importance, as those which this flippant superficial writer has selected for the object of his unseasonable gibes.

Hebrew manuscripts are of two sorts, the one written in the old or Samaritan, the other in the new or Chaldee characters. These are two collateral branches from the same stem; two copies of the same original instrument, under the guardianship of two different peoples*, jealous of one another, abominating one another; and, therefore, altogether unlikely to enter into any collusion. Yet, as both copies were the same at the beginning, they still remain so in all essentials; and reciprocally vouch for one another's authenticity. It was the saying of St. Augustine, that the Jews, through a particular dispensation of Providence, were the Christians book-keepers. In like manner, the Samaritans may be said to have been book-keepers to the Jews; and I will venture to affirm, that they have been the best keepers of the two. The Samaritan scripture, as far as it goes, (for it contains only the Pentateuch) must appear to every one, who examines it with any degree of attention, and void of rabbinical prepossessions, a far more faithful representative of the prototype, than any Masoretic copy, at this day extant.

It is, indeed, only of late, that we knew the full value of this long latent treasure. The first edition of it was published by Morinus, in the Paris polyglott, in the year 1645; and only from one manuscript. The variations of that manuscript, from the present Hebrew text, were reprinted more accurately, by Houbigant, in

---

* I have ventured, after B. Lowth, to use the plural of this word; which in some cases seems to be necessary, and is perfectly analogous.

1753. Since that time, feventeen other manufcripts have been collated, either in the whole, or in felect paffages; by the aid of which, the greateft part of the errors, that are in the firft printed copy, may be corrected; and the futile objections of Hottinger and his followers effectually obviated.

Although the Jewifh manufcripts are of lefs utility, in reftoring the true text, than the Samaritan; having been all written pofteriorly to the introduction of the Mafora; and, for the moft part, remodelled by the fame examplar of it; yet they afford many important readings, with regard to the fenfe; and of grammatical corrections a number almoft infinite. This laft advantage alone deferved all the labour and expence that have been beftowed in collating them; and the world is principally indebted to the liberality of this nation, and to the indefatigable perfeverance of the late Dr. Kennicott for fo ufeful a work. The prejudices at firft raifed againft it, by ignorance or miftaken zeal, are daily dying away; and its value muft rife, in the eftimation of the learned, in proportion as it is known and examined.

Notwithftanding Dr. Kennicott's various readings were collected from upwards of fix hundred manufcripts, and all the printed copies he could procure, yet the harveft is far from being over. A very large fupplement is promifed by De Roffi of Parma *, from

* The firft volume was publifhed laft year, 1784; and, befides a very fenfible preface, canons and *clavis*, contains various readings on the three firft books of Mofes. The fecond volume will be publifhed in the courfe of the prefent year.

more than four hundred manuscripts, some of which are said to be of the seventh or eighth century; as well as from a considerable number of rare and unnoted editions: and, no doubt, there will be still plentiful gleanings, even after De Rossi; especially, if ever the repositories of the East happen to be freely opened, and men of learning and enterprize be found to avail themselves of the occasion. Meanwhile, let us be heartily thankful for the riches we already possess, and employ them to the best advantage.

A-kin to the various readings of Hebrew manuscripts, and of much the same utility in correcting the Hebrew text, are the parallel places of the text itself; and the quotations made from it at different times, whether by Jewish or Christian writers *.

By parallel places, we mean those passages of Scripture, in which the same precept is reiterated; the same historical fact repeated; or the same canticle, psalm or prophecy, entirely or partially reinserted. When, in any of these cases, there is a manifest contradiction, or glaring inconsistency, between the two passages, we may conclude, that one of them, at least, is corrupted; and it is the province of criticism to determine, from circumstances, where the error and where the truth lies. Examples, not a few, may be seen in Houbigant, Kennicott, Starck, &c.

With regard to quotations; if we were sure, that they had al-

---

* We speak here only of such quotations as have been made from the original, whether exhibited in Hebrew characters, or in those of any other language.

ways been extracted from books, they might be considered as so many various readings, of equal estimation with those found in manuscripts of the same antiquity; but it may be suspected that they were, sometimes made from memory; and, therefore, they are to be examined with care, and adopted with caution. It cannot, however, be denied that they are frequently of use in restoring the true reading; and it were to be wished that a still more ample collection were made of them than has yet been done *.

Another most copious source of emendation of the Hebrew text, are the translations that have been made of it, at different periods, and in different languages; which, while they serve, in general, to evidence its authenticity, enable us, at the same time, to correct, or even restore many particular passages, that are now either entirely lost or strangely corrupted: an advantage which belongs not, in the same degree, to any other ancient writing.

To illustrate this by an example—It is well known, that Longinus's celebrated treatise on the sublime has come down to us erroneous and imperfect. But if it had been accurately translated into Latin, while it was yet intire and uncorrupted; and if many

* The various readings in the Talmud and other rabbinical writings were collected with great care by Gill, and inserted in Dr. Kennicott's Bible. Montfaucon had, long before, gathered what scattered fragments of this nature he could find among the Greek and Latin fathers, or in the margin of manuscript Bibles; and published them in his Hexapla in 1713. To these some additions were made by Bahrdt in 1769; and many more might still be made, if some new Montfaucon would arise, to ransack old parchments with the same industry and judgment.

ancient copies of that tranflation yet remained, it would be no difficult matter to reftore by them, in a great meafure, the true fenfe, if not always the very terms of the text of Longinus. Let us, now, fuppofe that, inftead of one Latin tranflation, we had three or four; and as many more in Greek, different only in dialect from that of the original; and that all thofe verfions were not only accurate and faithful, but ftrictly and even fervilely literal; in fuch a cafe, every one muft be fenfible, that it would be hard to avoid hitting upon the true text of the author*. That this cafe is fully applicable to the text of the Hebrew fcriptures will appear from the following concife account of the principal ancient verfions.

The firft of thefe, both in time and dignity, is that which we call the Septuagint or LXX. (it fhould be LXXII.) from the number of perfons, who, according to fome of the too credulous ancients, were employed in making it. The moft judicious critics now laugh, with St. Jerom, at the fable of Arifteas; yet they are not agreed among themfelves, about many queftions relative to this famous verfion. Without entering, at prefent, into a difcuffion of thofe knotty points, I fhall only fay, in very few words, what appears to me certain, or moft probable.

* The works of Ariftotle are much in the fame predicament with thofe of Longinus. The beft Greek editions of them are extremely imperfect, for want of good manufcripts. But, if we could recover compleat copies of the Syriac and Arabic verfions, which we know were made of them from the originals, it is not to be doubted that many of the erroneous and obfcure paffages of that ufeful author, would thereby be corrected or illuftrated. See B. Lowth's preface to Ifaiah.

Firſt then, That the Greek verſion, called the Septuagint, is not all the work of the ſame tranſlator or tranſlators, is manifeſt, from the very great diverſity of ſtile and the various modes of tranſlating, that prevail in it. The arguments from authority, produced in ſupport of the contrary opinion, need no other refutation, than a bare inſpection of the books themſelves: for who, that has ever looked into them, will venture to affirm, that the Pentateuch, Eccleſiaſtes, Amos, and Jeremiah were tranſlated by the ſame perſons? Not to mention that the moſt unexceptionable authorities, thoſe of Joſephus and Philo, are on the other ſide.

Secondly, The Pentateuch, or five books of Moſes, called emphatically the Law, ſeems to have been tranſlated in the reign, and, probably, at the requeſt of Ptolomy Philadelphus, by certain Jews of Alexandria; aſſiſted, perhaps, by ſome of their brethren from Paleſtine.

Thirdly, The other books were all tranſlated between that period and the birth of Chriſt; or, at leaſt, ſoon after: but where, by whom, or at what particular aera, we can, for the moſt part, form only vague conjectures.

At whatever time, or by whatever perſons the Greek verſion was compleated, it was certainly of great authority among the Helleniſt Jews, and, for a time, read in their ſynagogues inſtead of the Hebrew. To give it the higher degree of credit, and to juſtify an innovation which was not approved of by ſome of their brethren, the ridiculous tale of the feventy cells, &c. feems to have been invented. The Chriftians, who have, in all ages, been more or lefs the dupes of Rabbinifm, readily believed the ill-contrived ftory; and thence concluding, that the tranflators were infpired perfons, confidered their work not as a mere verfion, but as a fecond divine original *.

It was early tranflated into Latin, and became the text-book of the Weftern, as well as of the Eaftern churches. It was the only copy of the Scripture they generally ufed; and the only one they appealed to in all their controverfies. They particularly, and moft advantageoufly employed it in confuting the Jews themfelves, from whom they had received it; proving to them from it, by the moft irrefragable arguments, that their expected Meffias muft have already come, in the perfon of Jefus Chrift.

On this, even the Hellenift Jews began to entertain an unfavourable idea of it; and, at length, had it in fuch abhorrence, that a national faft was inftituted to deplore the fame event (the anniverfary of its being tranflated) which they had before commemorated by a folemn feftival. Whether this fudden change in their minds was altogether owing to the above circumftance, and their deeply-rooted hatred to the Chriftians; or whether it might not partly arife from the real differences, that were now found (no matter how

---

* This opinion was the prevailing one as late as the fifth century, and St. Jerom gave great offence by calling it in queftion.

they had come there) between it and the Hebrew text; or whether, in fine, the Christians, on their part, had, through a mistaken zeal, made some little alterations in it, to make it speak more explicitly the language of Christianity *, it is hard, at this day, to determine: but the fact is indisputable; and, even before the end of the first century, the Septuagint version was depreciated by every Jewish writer, and expelled from every synagogue.

It was to supply its place, that Aquila of Pontus, first a convert from Paganism to Christianity and then a proselyte to Judaism, undertook a new Greek version of the Bible for his new brethren. It appeared about the year 129, and was so well received by the Jews, that he was encouraged to give, soon after, a more correct edition of it, accompanied with a commentary, that rendered it still more palatable to them. On the other hand, the Christians reprobated it as a dangerous and disingenuous attempt to overthrow the authority of the Septuagint, and charged him with having wilfully corrupted, or mistranslated, even his own originals. The character given of him by St. Jerom, in whose time his version was extant, is not always the same. Sometimes † he calls him a contentious and captious interpreter, who affects to weigh words and syllables, and crowds his translation with unheard-of solecisms: at other times, ‡ he praises his diligence and exactitude; denies that

---

* Of this I think there is at least one example preserved by St. Jerom. *Comment. in Habbacuc.*
† Ep. ad Pammach.   ‡ Ep. ad Damasum.

he is so captious as he is called; and makes no scruple to prefer him to all other translators. To judge from the fragments that now remain, the first of these opinions is evidently the right one. He is an uncouth, barbarous writer, the Arias Montanus or Malvenda of his day; who seems to have purposely chosen that servile mode of translating, to hide the malevolence of his views, and to make his strict adherence to the letter of the Hebrew a plausible pretext, for deviating so widely from the old version. We regret, however, that his translation is lost, as it would have been singularly useful both for discovering the state of the Hebrew text at that time, and giving us the literal meaning and etymology of many words, the signification of which it is now difficult to ascertain; although, independently of these considerations, it was hardly worth the saving*.

Perhaps the Jews themselves were sensible of the too great servility, and consequent obscurity, of Aquila's version; and therefore wished to have another, that should be equally favourable to their prejudices, without being so unintelligible and disgusting. This, we may suppose, produced the translation of Theodotion,

* The loss of this version was chiefly owing to a cause that seemed rather calculated to preserve it. The Emperor Justinian, on forbidding the Talmud, now become the favourite book of the Jews, gave them full leave to use the version of Aquila, which they had formerly extolled as a faithful and accurate translation: but a sort of obstinacy, not entirely peculiar to Jews, urged them not only to reject with contempt what was thus freely offered to them; but even, probably, to destroy all the copies they could find of it; and which were mostly in their own possession.

which he published about the year 184. This writer, who had been first a disciple of Tatian, then a Marcionite, and lastly a Jew, retained as much of the old Alexandrian version, as he saw for his purpose; and only altered, added, or retrenched, where he found it differ from such Hebrew manuscripts, as the Jews put into his hands. This was a sly device, and operated according to his wish. The Jews were well pleased with his version, because it was conformable to their ideas; and the Christians were not offended, because it so much resembled the Septuagint. In many particular passages, and in one whole book*, they preferred it to the Septuagint itself; especially after Origen had made use of it to correct the supposed faults of the latter; in order to make it tally with, what he thought, the *Hebrew verity*. Hence it is, that much more of this version has been preserved, than of Aquila's.

Towards the end of the same century, or early in the next, appeared another Greek translation, less literal and infinitely more elegant, than either of the foregoing ones. It was the work of Symmachus; who, if we may believe Eusebius, from being a Samaritan, became a Jew; from being a Jew, a Christian; and from being a Christian, an Ebionite. In this last communion, and for the use of its members, he composed his work, which he afterwards seems to have remodelled, in a second edition. The version of Symmachus is, often and deservedly, praised by Eusebius and St. Jerom;

---

* Daniel.

and the latter seems to have made it, in a great measure, the pattern of his Latin translation. It was, indeed, remarkable for its perspicuity and propriety, as well as elegance; and no good reason can be assigned for its not having been more generally adopted, but that its author belonged to a sect, who were equally hateful to both Jews and Christians. Many excellent works have perished from a similar cause.

Besides these Greek versions of the Old Testament, there are three others mentioned by the ancient fathers; called the *fifth*, *sixth*, and *seventh*; because their respective authors or editors are not known. They seem to have comprehended only, or chiefly, the poetical books of Scripture. Whether they were made by Jews or Christians, it is hard to say; although the sixth bears strong marks of Christian extraction; or, perhaps, it was only an interpolated edition of the Septuagint*.

However that be, it is certain that all those versions were collected by the indefatigable Origen, and placed, together with the Septuagint and original Hebrew text, in his famous Hexapla: and this, perhaps, is the last entire copy of them that ever was made. For the Talmudists having gradually excluded all Greek versions from the synagogues, and the Christians universally adhering to the old translation, the rest were either totally neglected; or only such parts of them copied into the margents of Bibles and com-

---

* This may, one day, be the subject of a particular discussion.

mentaries, as were deemed the moſt worthy of attention*. Thus it was that the Septuagint verſion triumphed, at length, over all its rivals, and remained, for ſeveral ages after, the ſole Scripture ſtandard in all the Chriſtian churches †.

We are not, however, to imagine, that it was exactly the ſame in every church, or that any church poſſeſſed a copy of it that was perfectly correct; much leſs, that any ſuch copy now exiſts. It had contracted many blemiſhes in the days of Origen; and it was principally with a view to remove them, that he deſigned and executed the moſt celebrated of all his works. No man could be better qualified for ſuch an undertaking; to a ſtrong conſtitution, a clear head and a moſt prodigious memory, he had joined an immenſe and univerſal erudition, by the moſt aſſiduous and inceſſant application that, perhaps, ever was made. His inſatiable thirſt for learning made him pry into every corner, for rare and curious books; and the liberality of his rich friends put it in his power to purchaſe them.

With all theſe advantages, he begun, about the year 231, to compile his *Tetrapla*; which contained, in ſo many ſeparate co-

* Of all ſuch fragments Montfaucon compoſed his Hexapla; a book indiſpenſibly neceſſary to every Biblical ſtudent; and of which a new and more compleat edition is greatly wanted.

† The reader who wiſhes to form a proper idea of the Septuagint verſion, will do well to conſult Hody *de textibus originalibus*, &c. *Voſſius de 70 interpretibus*, Grabe's *Prolegomena* to his edition of the Alexandrian manuſcript, and *De variis vitiis*, &c. Father Simon's *Critical hiſtory of the Old Teſtament*, Fabricy's *Titres primitifs*, and Doctor Owen's excellent *Diſſertation* publiſhed a few years ago.

lumns, and in the following order, the four Greek verfions of Aquila, Symmachus, the Septuagint and Theodotion. It would have been well, perhaps, if he had contented himfelf with this firft laborious compilation; which was alone fufficient to immortalize his name, and would have been much more eafily handed down to pofterity, than the great and over-grown work that fuperfeded it. It would have been even more ufeful; for as yet he had not affumed the province of correcting the text of the Septuagint; but had given it, juft as he found it, from the beft manufcripts he could procure.

But the very confiderable differences, which he could not but obferve, between it and the three other verfions, fo lately made from the originals, and fo nearly agreeing with one another, made him fufpect that it was much more erroneous than he had formerly thought it; and fet him on meditating a work that fhould, both by its magnitude and importance, totally eclipfe the former one. This produced, in fucceffion, the *Hexapla, Octapla* and *Enneapla;* fo denominated from the number of columns, that each contained. In the *Enneapla*, which had nine columns, the three laft contained the three anonymous Greek verfions before-mentioned; the four, immediately preceding them, were the fame with thofe of the *Tetrapla*; and, in the two firft, ftood the original text in Hebrew letters, with its pronounciation by its fide in Greek characters: both, fuch as he received them from the Jews: for his knowledge of the Hebrew was, by far, too scanty, to enable him to do without them; and he never suspected, that they might, possibly, impose upon him; any more than St. Jerom did, afterwards, on a like occasion.

Emboldened by his new guides, he ventured now to *slash with his desperate hook* the venerable texture of the old version; and to patch and piece it, with the more recent manufacture of Theodotion, much in the same manner as Clarius and some other moderns have patched the Vulgate *. This had bad consequences. The great authority of Origen made every one, who was possessed of a Greek Bible, revise his copy by the Hexaplar standard; and, in a short time, no manuscript, that was not bristled over with asterisks and obelisks, lemnisks and hypolemnisks, was accounted of any value.

If the autograph of Origen still remained, or if the art of printing had then existed, to circulate at once a great number of accurate copies, we should have less reason to complain of the confusion that thence ensued. His distinguishing marks, without adulterating the Septuagint, would have indicated the then state of the Hebrew text, and put it in our power, even at this day, to appretiate both †: whereas, through the carelessness of ignorant transcri-

---

* *Sed, quod majoris audaciae est, in editione Septuaginti Theodotionis editionem miscuit.* Hieron. praef. in Paralip.

† *Et haec quidem signa, si studiose semper a librariis servata, essent in manuscriptis, non exiguum inde fructum caperet Critica sacra; at nox, pro librariorum socordia et negligentia, omissa sunt; unde maxima in libris Graecis orta est confusio.* Starck, *Davidis Carm.* vol. 1. p. 152.

bers, or the caprice of future correctors, the disorder grew every day greater and greater; until, at length, it became irremediable.

For other persons, less capable than Origen or his editors Pamphilus and Eusebius, set about correcting the *common* * copies, after their example. The principal of these were Lucianus and Hesychius, whose authority, whatever might be their abilities, vied almost equally with Origen's. The exemplar corrected by Lucianus was used in all the churches from Antioch to Constantinople. At Alexandria, and all over Egypt, the corrections of Hesychius were adopted; while the Christians of Palestine stuck tenaciously to the Pamphilian copy of the Hexapla †; which, in the end, seems to have generally prevailed through all the East.

From which of those copies, or editions, the particular manuscripts, now extant in different parts of the world, are derived; and what manuscript deviates least from the old original version, it is impossible to determine, or even to guess, until the manuscripts themselves be collated and compared. This is, at present, the greatest *desideratum* in sacred philology; and had the Author of this Prospectus a fortune sufficient to travel for that purpose, he would think it well employed, were it equal to that of Croesus: nor should his present undertaking, great as it is, prevent him from execut-

---

* The uncorrected edition of the Septuagint was, after the days of Origen, known by the name of *common*, κοινη as we call, now, the Latin version of Jerom, the Vulgate.

† Hieron. ad Chromat. cvii.

ing a project so nearly connected with it; and from which it would, undoubtedly, derive a greater degree of perfection *. Meanwhile, we must make the best use we can of the printed editions, and of such various readings of manuscripts as we can procure: not neglecting even the secondary translations that have any degree of antiquity †.

We have four different edited exemplars of the Greek version; That of Alcala or the Complutensian, that of Venice or the Aldine, that of Rome, and that of Oxford.

The first was printed in the polyglott Bible of Ximenes in the year 1515, with a typothetical attention, that would put the most patient modern compositor in a rage. It is accompanied with an

* I have been told that a very learned gentleman of the University of Cambrige had, some time ago, expressed his readiness to undertake such a work, if he should meet with due encouragement. Is it possible that he has not, or will not meet with due encouragement, in a country, where the most trifling novelty draws, every season, from the purses of the good people of England, a far greater sum than would be adequate to the purpose? With five thousand pounds, I would, undertake, in less than three years, to collate every valuable Greek manuscript of the Bible in Europe.

† Great hopes are entertained of being able, in some measure, to restore Origen's copy of the Septuagint, together with the other Greek versions that composed his Tetrapla; by means of a Syriac version, made from them in the seventh century; a considerable part of which is preserved in the Ambrosian library at Milan. It contains the Prophets and *Agiographa*. The first part of this manuscript is, with great probability, said to have been once in the possession of Masius; and from it he drew his Hexaplar readings, in his commentary on Joshua: but what is since become of it, no one, it seems, can tell. Even then it had been mutilated of the Pentateuch; of which, however, there is an Arabic version, in the Bodleian library at Oxford. May we not expect the publication of this Pentateuch, from the zeal and abilities of the present Arabic Professor? That, with Mr. Norberg's transcript from the Ambrosian volume, would be a most valuable present to the Biblical student. See Professor White's letter to the Bishop of London; or Bp. Newcome's preface to the minor Poets.

interlineary verbal tranſlation, and is of all the Greek editions the moſt conſonant with the preſent Hebrew text. The editors boaſt of ancient manuſcripts, and ancient manuſcripts they ſurely had; but, as they neither tell what thoſe were, nor how they uſed them, we draw little ſatisfaction from this general information. It is even juſtly ſuſpected, that they did not ſcrupulouſly adhere to ſuch manuſcripts as they had; but that, to make their edition correſpond, as nearly as poſſible, with the Hebrew and Vulgate, with which it was claſſed in the ſame page, they gleaned from every quarter a medley of a verſion, that was neither one thing nor another. It is aſtoniſhing that ſuch a copy ſhould have been republiſhed in the Antwerp and Paris polyglotts.

The edition of Venice was firſt publiſhed in the year 1518, by the heirs of Aldus. It was profeſſedly printed from very old, but undeſcribed manuſcripts; with which however its editors ſeem not to have taken the ſame freedom, as thoſe of Alcala had taken with theirs. It is, evidently a much purer copy of the Septuagint; although not without many foreign admixtures; eſpecially from Theodotion. It has been often reprinted, with variations and pretended corrections; ſometimes for the worſe. The beſt editions of it, beſide that of Venice, are thoſe of Baſil and Frankfort.

The Roman edition, begun in the pontificate of Gregory XIII. and compleated in that of Sixtus V. (who while a cardinal had preſſingly urged the work) appeared in the year 1587. It was principally taken from the famous Vatican manuscript; and, where it failed, from others of nearly the same antiquity; and is, by many, thought to be the most genuine copy of the old Greek version, that has yet been published. Had the learned editors been more attentive, to exhibit their prototypes exactly as they found them; we should have been still better pleased with their labours: for it is now certain, that they sometimes deviated from their manuscripts; but uncertain, where and how much they deviated. It has been lately proposed to the present Pope, to have the Vatican manuscript republished, exactly as it is; and even in the same form and characters; and it is with the greatest pleasure we learn that his Holiness has not only approved of the proposal, but has also taken upon himself the whole expence of the impression. This does great honour to Pius VI. and will contribute more to immortalize his memory, than any other event of his reign; his journey to Vienna not excepted *.

The Roman edition, together with Nobilius's Latin version, first separately published in the year 1588, was, by order and at the expence of the Gallican clergy, reprinted at Paris, under the inspection of Morinus, in the year 1626; and again in 1641. We are

* We are just now informed, but hope the information is false, that this most laudable design has been traversed by the Roman inquisitors; and that, through the councils of a Greek bigot, the Vatican manuscripts are, in future, to lie on their dusty shelves, untouched and unexplored. If this be true, Ghosts of Carafa, Paßionei, Spinelli, Assemanni, arise! and drive these Goths and Vandals from the precincts of your old dominion.

certainly indebted to the zeal of the French Bishops for procuring so elegant and correct an edition of a book that had become extremely rare, and was hardly to be purchased: but the obligation is considerably diminished, if it be true, as Serravius and others affirm, that this edition prevented Ducaeus from giving the infinitely more useful one he meditated *.

When Walton published the London polyglott in the year 1657, he judiciously adopted the Roman edition of the Greek version, instead of the Complutensian; and this, with other things, contributed to give his polyglott a decided superiority over all the rest. It was also republished at Francker by Bos in the year 1709, in one thick quarto volume; and again at Utrecht and Amsterdam by Millius in 1728, in two volumes, small octavo.—All the other editions of London, Cambridge, Amsterdam, Leipsick, &c, are spurious, and most grossly interpolated.

The last, but not the least important, edited exemplar of the Septuagint, is that which was printed from the celebrated Alexandrian manuscript in the British Musaeum; of equal antiquity with that of the Vatican, and, in some respects, more valuable.

* Fronto Ducaeus (Fronton le Duc) a Jesuit of Bourdeaux, the most learned editor of the first Greek and Latin Chrysostome, and one of the best critics of his age, had planned, it seems, a new edition of the Septuagint; in which it was his intention to restore, if possible, the genuine exemplar of Origen, with all its diacritic marks: but the Parisian editors of the Roman exemplar, alarmed at the project, which would in effect have impeded the sale of their copies, did all they could to counteract it, and were unluckily but too successful. The materials which he had prepared were ordered to Rome, and have never since been heard of.

It was prepared for the press by Grabe, with a care and candor that have not often been equalled, never surpassed; but which, we trust, will be henceforth faithfully imitated by every editor of manuscripts. The first and fourth volumes were, by Grabe himself, published at Oxford in folio and octavo in the years 1707 and 1709; the second and third by Lee and Shippen, with the assistance of Bishop Potter in 1719—20. It was immediately republished at Leipsick by Reineccius, in 1712, &c; but the most commodious edition of it is that of Zurick, by Breitinger, in 1730. Until the Romans are pleased to give us more correct copy of their manuscript, this edition must be our text-book of the Greek version; and all future collations of manuscripts should be made relatively to it *.

With regard to the various readings already collated, the greatest part of which have been crowded together in the lower margin of Bos's edition, they are not implicitly to be depended on; even when extracted from printed books. In every dubious passage, the editions themselves are to be consulted, and the typographical errors of these always taken into consideration. Of manuscripts, indeed, few general and continued collations have yet been made. The variations of the very ancient Cottonian fragment, now lost, were carefully collated by Grabe, and accurately published by Dr.

* Professor White of Oxford, so well known by his elegant and affecting lectures, has in a letter to the Bishop of London, in 1779, laid down some excellent rules for having a good new edition of the Septuagint; a work very much wanted; and which we wish the learned professor's other avocations would permit him to undertake.

PROSPECTUS.

Owen in the year 1778: Dr. Kennicott had collated for his own use several parts of the principal manuscripts at Oxford, and of an old Psaltery at Eton: it is hoped they are not lost *. Mr. Woide, at the request of Bishop Lowth, collated, through the book of Isaiah, two valuable manuscripts in the British Musaeum; one of them, through Jeremiah, for Mr. Blayney; and through the minor Prophets, for B. Newcome. The Author of this Prospectus hopes to procure, both at home and abroad, some similar assistance †; and we expect soon to hear of Birch and Adler having published their copious collections.

It has been said, that we ought not to neglect the ancient versions, that have been made from the Septuagint. Of these the most celebrated is the Latin *Italic*, which chiefly prevailed in all the Western churches during the five first centuries. If an entire and unadulterated copy of this version existed, it would be little less valuable than the Septuagint itself. What parts of it could be found have been collected by Nobilius, Blanchini and Sabbatier.

There are also Syriac, Samaritan, Ethiopic, Arabic and Armenian translations from the Greek, partly printed, but chiefly in

---

* I have, since writing this, been assured by the Bishop of Salisbury, to whom and the Dean of Christ-church Dr. Kennicott left his papers, that no such collections are found among them.

† While these sheets are printing, I am actually employed in collating a valuable and well-preserved Octateuch, belonging to the University of Glasgow; a particular account of which shall in due time be given to the public.

manuscript; which have their respective uses, towards the same purpose, according to their antiquity and accuracy, and certainly deserve to be made known and appretiated.

But of all the versions made from the Septuagint the Coptic is by far the most useful; both because it is a strictly verbal translation, and because it is of great antiquity. Wilkins published the Pentateuch from three manuscripts in the year 1731. But much, much yet remains to be done; and the arduous task seems to be reserved for Mr. Woide. He is, perhaps, the only man in Europe, who is fully equal to it; and when he has compleated the singular work he has now in hand *, he will, no doubt, be encouraged to set about it †.

Having said this much on the different Greek versions of the Bible ‡, and of their utility in restoring the true readings of the original text, we proceed to the other ancient translations; at the head of which is to be placed the Syriac.

That the Syrians had a version of the scripture, at a very early

* A *Fac-simile* of the New Testament of the Alexandrian manuscript; the most curious piece of workmanship that ever came from the press, now happily compleated.

† He has, with unremitted industry, already procured several Coptic fragments; and expects more from the friendship of the prelate Borgia, the present most learned and amiable prefect of the *Propaganda*; whose zeal to discover, and readiness to communicate useful old writings of every kind, are perfectly congenial to Mr. Woide's own disposition.

‡ Mr. Villoison discovered lately a Greek version of the Bible, in St. Mark's library at Venice, entirely different from that of the Septuagint; but, as it has not yet been published, we cannot form a proper judgment of it. It has, however, all the appearance of being a much more modern translation, than even that of Symmachus.

period, is indifputable; although the tradition, that carries it back to the reign of Solomon, deferves no credit. As it is mentioned by the Greek writers of the fecond century, it muft have been then generally known; and may, therefore, without temerity, be afcribed to the apoftolic age. Hence it is evident, that a genuine copy of it would be highly valuable; as it would, not only point out the changes which the Hebrew text may have undergone, from the time it had been firft tranflated into Greek; but, alfo, ferve to corroborate many good readings, and correct many bad ones, of both the Greek tranflation, and the Hebrew original. In this laft refpect, it would be more ufeful than any other verfion. Of all the Oriental dialects, the Syriac approaches the nigheft to the Hebrew; and the Syriac tranflator follows his text fo clofely and literally, that he may be faid to give a tranfcript, rather than a tranflation. But his work has had the fate of all ancient books: it has come down to us greatly disfigured, by the negligence of copyifts, and the audacity of pretended correctors. It was publifhed, not very faithfully, by Gabriel Sionita, in the Paris polyglott, from a manufcript in the French king's library. The editors of the London polyglott had it partly corrected on three other exemplars: but it is ftill exceedingly faulty *, and a collation of it with all the manufcripts that can be found, and with the writings of the ancient Syriac fathers, is ex-

---

* Several letters of the Syriac alphabet are more eafily miftaken for one another, than even thofe of the Hebrew; and this has been one moft fertile fource of errors.

tremely defirable. I have hopes, that the gentlemen of the Maronite college at Rome may be prevailed upon to undertake a confiderable fhare of fo ufeful a work *.

Of much the fame affinity of idiom to the Hebrew with the Syriac, are the Chaldee verfions; made for the ufe of the Jews, after the Hebrew had ceafed to be a living language. Thefe are of various forts and different qualities, from the fervile tranflation to the loofeft paraphrafe; and from an almoft pure Babylonifh dialect to the moft barbarous rabbinical jargon. They are not, confequently, all of the fame utility: yet the very worft of them will be found to have its ufe; and, even from the dunghill of the Jerufalem Targum, a pearl may be here and there picked up. The moft ancient and accurate is that of Onkelos, who tranflated only the Pentateuch. From a refemblance of name, he has been confounded with Aquila, the author of the Greek verfion. The Rabbins, indeed, will have their Onkelos to be much more ancient; but there is fome reafon to think he muft have been of a ftill latter date. Be that as it may, he fticks clofely to his text; which, it is evident, could not, in many places, be the fame with our prefent Maforetic copies. Next to him in rank, but at a great diftance, ftands Jonathan with his Targums. The reft are an obfcure and anonymous herd; who feem to vie with one another, which fhall advance the greateft abfurdi-

* See the note † page 34.

ties. The least ridiculous among them are they, who paraphrased the Psalms and Proverbs.

Although the Arabic versions, at least such of them as have been made from the Hebrew, are of a much latter period than the other Oriental translations; and, therefore, not of the same utility for correcting the originals; yet we cannot subscribe to the opinion of those, who think them of little or no use at all, for that purpose. The version of Saadias * is as old as the tenth century; and exhibits a faithful though not verbal translation of the Hebrew copies he worked upon. I have found some excellent readings in it; and I wonder that Houbigant should have preferred to it the novel and barbarous African version published by Erpenius. The African version, however, is not without its use. Being extremely literal, it gives us a good idea of the state of the Hebrew text, at the time of its being made; and furnishes us with many etymological helps to discover the meaning of obscure Hebrew words. But a more valuable Arabic version than either of these, made from the Samaritan Pentateuch, lies yet in manuscript; of which a specimen from the Barberini triglott was published by Hwiid in the year 1780.

---

* I do not here enter into a discussion of those much agitated questions. Whether the Arabic version in our polyglotts be a primary or a secondary translation? whether Saadias-Gaon be the same with Saïd of Fiumi? or whether he translated only the Pentateuch? These points will probably be the subject of a particular dissertation. It is enough for me at present, that the Arabic version has, partly at least, been certainly either made from, or retouched upon the originals.

There are several other copies of it in Europe; and we join our warmest wishes to those of F. Georgi *, that the joint labours of the learned of all countries and communions may soon give us a compleat edition of it. Let F. Georgi himself set the example by procuring a collation of the manuscripts of Italy; which in his present station, he can easily do†. The rest seems to be destined for Woide or Maidenhover ‡.

We come now to the famous Latin Vulgate, which, for eleven hundred years, was the general text-book of all the Western churches; and is still the public Scripture standard, in those of the Roman communion. The first Latin versions of the Bible were made from the Greek of the Septuagint, and as the Greek copies greatly varied, the Latin versions varied still more; because they were not only done from different architypes, but also by many different hands: for every one, says St. Augustine, who had got a tincture of Greek learning, fell to translating for himself; so that before the end of the fourth century, the translations had become innumerable ‖.

To remedy this glaring inconvenience, St. Jerom undertook to

---

* See his elegant letter to Hwiid, printed with the above specimen.

† I believe he is now General of the order of Dominican Friars.

‡ I am just now told that this gentleman, well known for his German translation of Job, has already collated some of the Arabic manuscripts at Oxford; and continues to enrich his collection from other libraries, particularly those of Spain.

‖ See St. Augustine *De doctrina Christiana*, lib. ii. cap. 2.

revife that which was chiefly ufed, and known by the name of *Italic*, on the moft correct copies of the Greek. Having now occafion to confult the works of Origen he foon perceived that the Greek itfelf was in many places corrupted; or, at leaft, that it differed widely from the Greek verfions, that had been more recently made from the Hebrew; and this it probably was, that gave him the firft idea of the neceffity of a new tranflation. For that purpofe, he applied eagerly to the ftudy of the Hebrew language, confulted the moft learned of the Jewifh doctors, compared all the Greek verfions with one another and with the original; and, at length, convinced of the infufficiency of the old Latin verfion, even with all his own corrections and improvements, he ferioufly fet about making a new one, from the beft Hebrew copies he could procure. This he accomplifhed at different intervals, and rather by ftarts than a continued labour, in the fpace of fifteen years; amidft many contradictions, reproaches, and the moft bitter invectives.

For .fcarcely had his firft effays made their appearance, when the cry from every quarter was fet up againft them, as a daring and dangerous innovation; that tended to difcredit a verfion fo long ufed in the Latin church, and made from one generally believed to have been the work of the Holy Ghoft.

Although Jerom, confcious of the rectitude of his intentions and of the goodnefs of his caufe, defpifed, at firft, the unjuft and invidious cavils of his adversaries; yet they were so often repeated, and countenanced by such high characters in the church, that he was fain to yield to the necessity of the times, and to make apology after apology for his conduct. Still, however, he continued to translate, without following any other order than what the requests of his particular friends occasionally suggested to him. The four books of Kings were first published in the year 391; soon after followed the Prophets; then the books of Solomon, Job, the Psalms, Ezra, Nehemiah, Chronicles; and, last of all, the Octateuch *, about the year 405. By this time, the storm, that had been raised against him, was nearly blown over; and he lived to see his labours applauded by some of those who had been the first to condemn them. In less than a century after his death his version had become of equal authority with its now only rival, the Italic; and gradually grew in estimation, till, at length, it was, with some limitations, universally adopted by the Latin churches.

In many respects it deserved that preference. It had been made immediately from the original; by one who had every necessary qualification for such an undertaking. His learning, whether sacred or profane, was not less extensive than Origen's; his judgment and taste were more correct and exquisite. He had a perfect knowledge of the Greek and Latin languages; and was sufficiently ver-

---

* The five books of Moses, Joshua, Judges and Ruth.

fed in the Hebrew *. He had correct copies of the Hexapla, if not the autograph itself, before him. He was at no great diftance from a famous fchool of Jewifh Rabbins, whom he might confult as he faw occafion. He had traverfed the land with his own feet, and feen with his own eyes the principal places mentioned in facred hiftory. He was acquainted with the manners and cuftoms of the country. He knew its plants, its animals and its other productions. With all thefe advantages, and his fuperior talents, it was impoffible he fhould not fucceed. He adopted, in general, that mode of tranflating, which had been before fo much admired in Symmachus; and which, indeed, is the beft calculated to exprefs the full meaning of the original, without either hurting its integrity, or transferring its idiotifms. His ftile is plain, eafy and unaffected; and, although his Latinity is not that of the Auguftan age, it is neither barbarous nor inelegant. In his diction and phrafeology there is a peculiar grace and noble fimplicity, which it is not eafy to imitate; and which no other Latin verfion, except that of Houbigant, in any degree poffeffes.

The work of St. Jerom is not, however, completely perfect: alas! what work of man ever was? He frequently renders not all his text,

* St. Jerom's great knowledge of the Hebrew has been called in queftion by Le Clerc, and warmly afferted by Martianay and others; who, in their zeal for the honour of the holy doctor, forgot, fometimes, the rules of good breeding. Le Clerc's affertions were to be combated by reafonings, not by injuries. St. Jerom certainly knew more of the Hebrew language than any other Weftern Chriftian of his day: he knew much more than Origen; but he was inferior, in that refpect, to many moderns.

he sometimes gives more than it contains, and he not seldom mistakes its meaning. For the sake of perspicuity he is often too diffuse, and for the sake of brevity he is sometimes obscure. He changes proper names into appellatives, and appellatives into proper names. He makes improper divisions of colons and periods; and, on some occasions, he is either careless or hasty *. Add to this, that he seems not to have been always guided by the same rules of translating. Hence, there is a remarkable want of uniformity throughout: some parts being translated more, others less literally; and some even bordering on paraphrase. But still the greatest imperfection of St. Jerom's version arises from too great a confidence in his Jewish guides, and from his being prepossest with an idea, that the Hebrew copies were then absolutely faultless. This leads him to blame the Septuagint in many places, where they are not blameable, and where they read and render better than he. But whatever little original flaws may be in this jewel, it is still a gem of great value; and we are perfectly agreed with F. Fabricy, as to the propriety and importance of hav-

---

* It is astonishing with what rapidity he struck off his translations. The three books of Solomon he calls " the works of three days." That of Tobias he finished in one, although he had it to translate out of a language he did not well know, through the medium of another that was more familiar to him. Such dispatch in a modern translator would be deemed downright precipitation. But this circumstance, while it accounts for some negligences and oversights, is the strongest proof of his comprehensive genius, quick conceptions, and the most wonderful facility in writing that has ever been known. Erasmus, perhaps, came the nighest to him in all these respects.

ing the dirt and ſtraws, that have in the courſe of time ſtuck to it and obſcured its luſtre, effectually wiped away. This can be done only by a collation of manuſcripts, and I know no body of men more proper to undertake the work, than the learned of F. Fabricy's own order.

When the Weſtern churches adopted St. Jerom's verſion, they did not adopt it without reſerve. Many particular parts and ſome whole books of the Italic were ſtill retained; and ſeveral corrections from Aquila, Theodotion and Symmachus, as well as from the Maſoretic Hebrew were occaſionally introduced. This medley obtained, from its general reception, the name of Vulgate.

It has undergone many corrections and alterations at different periods. Towards the end of the eighth century it was reviſed by Alcuin at the deſire of Charlemagne. In the twelfth it was, with the aſſiſtance of ſome Jews, made more conformable to the Hebrew by Stephen abbot of Citeaux *. It was again, in the next age, corrected with great care and labour by the French Dominicans; and enriched with a number of various readings, not only from Latin manuſcripts, but alſo from the Hebrew and Greek copies †. This moſt uſeful work, by that conjunctive and ſubordinate induſ-

---

* Ciſtertium.

† The autograph of this *correctorium* is to be ſeen in the library of the Dominicans, ruë St. *Jacques*, Paris. A good account of it is given by Fabricy (Titres primitiſs tom. 11. p. 132.) It is to be regretted that the project of making a fair copy of it, formed in 1749, did not take place; though it is not doubted but it will be reſumed and executed in the beſt manner.

try that diftinguiſhes religious focieties, was foon multiplied or abridged over all the Order; and was confidered as a fort of canon to correct other manufcripts by.

Whether they, who gave the firſt printed edition at Mayence in the year 1462, ufed it; or what manufcript ferved them for an architype, it is not known. One thing is certain; the firſt printed editions are extremely faulty. That which was publiſhed in the year 1515, in the Complutenfian polyglott, is more correct than any that preceded it; but as the corrections were not always made on the authority of manufcripts, and as the editors have not told us what other fources they drew from, we read it with doubt and diftruft. The firſt who gave a good copy of the Vulgate was the celebrated Robert Stevens. All his editions are correct and beautiful; but that of 1540 is fuperlatively fo. It was made from fourteen defcribed manufcripts, and the three principal printed editions of Mayence, Bafil and Alcala. It was republiſhed with fome alterations by Hentennius in 1547; with various readings from thirty manufcripts; which are accurately defcribed. Hentennius's edition was improved by Lucas Brugenfis; and publiſhed, with his long promifed annotations, in 1580; and again, more fplendidly, in 1583 *.

Seventeen years were now elapfed fince the Council of Trent had

---

* Of the fame year, there is an elegant and commodious edition of it in fmall octavo. Both are by Plantin.

decreed the Vulgate to be an authentic copy of Scripture; and ordered it to be henceforth (exclusively of all other Latin versions) universally used and appealed to. The charge of having it carefully corrected, and accurately printed, was committed to the Roman Pontif; but little had been done during the troublesome reigns of Pius IV. and Pius V. so that Sixtus V. who was born for great things, had the honour of executing the great commission. He had already, as has been said, given an excellent edition of the Greek version of the Septuagint, in 1587; and he now gave, in 1590 * the first entire Latin Bible that was published by papal authority.

But neither papal authority itself, nor the anathemas denounced against those who should presume to alter the smallest particle of it, could procure it a long duration. The imperious and unpopular Sixtus was hardly cold in his grave, when the copies of his edition were called in and suppressed †; and a new one, with above two thousand alterations, was published, in 1592, by Clement VIII. of which all the other editions, that have since been made, are literal copies ‡.

* The bull of publication is dated in 1589, but the book was not made public till the year after.

† It was pretended that Sixtus himself had resolved on the suppression; but of this there is no proof, and little probability.

‡ When I say *literal* copies, I do not mean that there have been no changes made in the Vulgate, since the Clementine edition. It is well known that many little corrections, and

PROSPECTUS.

As to the respective merits of those two editions, the last is certainly more correct and more agreeable to the present copies of the originals; but the first seems to retain more of the old Vulgate, and to be better supported by the authority of manuscripts *. This was probably one of the reasons that induced the Clementine editors to exclude all various readings. Bellarmine was for giving them; but he was over-ruled by his fellow-labourers †. The c-mission was partly supplied in some posterior editions; but the amendments that had been pointed out by Bellarmine and others, have from time to time been admitted, even into the Vatican impressions; and thence have found their way into most other posterior editions.

* Dr. James, in his *Bellum Papale*, made a minute and invidious collation of the two editions of Sixtus and Clement; from which he and others have drawn conclusions not very favourable to the Roman See. But when the very most they ask is granted them, and when it is allowed that neither of the editions are faultless, does it follow that the Vulgate is not still a most respectable translation; or that the council were in the wrong to prefer it to all other Latin versions, that had yet appeared? I shall have frequent occasions to justify it against the cavils of Amana and other such supercilious and contentious critics; and to shew that it is, in many particular passages, a more genuine copy of Scripture than the present Masoretic text. Indeed the outragious attacks, made on this famous version by some, not the most judicious, Protestant writers, may have, partly, arisen from a desire of retorting on such indiscreet Catholics, as had thrown unmerited abuse on the original. At present, the learned of both sides are in a fair way of being reconciled, in this one point at least; and seem willing to make mutual concessions. The Catholics are ready to own that the Vulgate is not so pure a rivulet, as some of their too zealous predecessors maintained; and the Protestants as readily acknowledge that the present Hebrew text is not so untainted a source as was long believed. Thus both contribute, in different ways, towards a reestablishment of the true text. Those without hesitation correct the Vulgate by the original, where the Vulgate is evidently faulty; and these make no scruple to make use of the Vulgate in restoring the true text of the original, when the original is evidently or probably corrupted.

† See his letter to Lucas Brugensis.

moſt ample and valuable collection was publiſhed at Antwerp by Lucas Brugenſis in the year 1618: and has ſince been frequently republiſhed, although never ſo correctly. Of latter years, ſince the collation of manuſcripts has been revived, ſome of the beſt Biblical critics have occaſionally had recourſe to thoſe of the Vulgate; and many good readings have been ſelected from them in particular books and paſſages. But a more general collation is ſtill wanted. When that has been accompliſhed, we doubt not but ſome zealous pope will ſee the expediency of having the Clementine edition again reviſed, and made more ſtrictly conformable to the originals, wherever there is no well grounded ſuſpicion of their being corrupted.

A third ſource of emendation of the Hebrew text of the Old Teſtament, are the quotations from it in the New. Theſe by ſome are ranked with the parallel places above-mentioned, to which indeed they have a great affinity. They differ, however, in the following reſpects. Firſt, they are in a different language. Secondly, they are not always made from the original; but more frequently from the Septuagint; and often, probably, from other early verſions. Thirdly, they are ſometimes quoted in ſo vague a manner, that we are at a loſs to know whence they were taken; or whether they were meant as ſtrict quotations, or ſimple inferences. As a ſource of emendation, therefore, they are to be uſed with great circumſpection; and the various readings, that may ſeem to ariſe from them, are rarely to be adopted; and not till every circumſtance has been weighed with an equal and patient hand. With theſe precautions, they may be of confiderable uſe; and we are greatly obliged to Dr. Randolph, for giving us ſo accurate a collation of them with the Hebrew text and Septuagint verſion. It was publiſhed at Oxford, with his learned annotations, in the year 1782.

The writings of Philo and Joſephus, the two principal Jewiſh authors of antiquity, after thoſe of the Scripture, have alſo been reckoned among the ſources from which ſome corrections of the Hebrew text may be drawn. The former, who was cotemporary with Jeſus Chriſt, cites, indeed, many paſſages of Holy writ; but as he was an Helleniſt of Alexandria, and evidently but little acquainted with the Hebrew dialect, we may ſuppoſe he followed the Septuagint; and therefore, although his quotations are uſeful, for corroborating or correcting the readings of that verſion, they can be but of ſecond hand utility towards the amendment of the original.

Not ſo with regard to Joſephus. He has given us a continued hiſtory of the Jews, extracted from the Hebrew copies of their own canonical books; and, at firſt, partly written by him in the Hebrew language. Now, although it is not improbable that he had alſo before him the Septuagint verſion, when he compoſed his Greek hiſtory, we cannot ſuppoſe that he would, on any account, prefer it to his originals; and the only fair concluſion we can draw from his difagreeing with our prefent Hebrew text, where he agrees with the Septuagint, is that our prefent Hebrew text and his Hebrew text are not the fame: confequently, where he depofes againft the prefent text in favour of the Septuagint, there is great reafon to fufpect that the former is corrupted. I fay, reafon to fufpect; for it by no means amounts to a certain proof; both becaufe the texts of Jofephus and of the Septuagint have their corruptions too; and becaufe there is a probability, at leaft, of fuch copies, as we now have of the one having been in fome places retouched, and made agreeable to thofe of the other. It is pretty plain, however, that this is not always the cafe; and it has been clearly fhewn by Kennicott and others that the work of Jofephus is often a ufeful commentary, fometimes a good *correctorium* of the Hebrew fcriptures—Let me add, that it forms a precious link in the long chain of evidence, that fupports their authenticity.

In fine, when the corruptions of the text cannot be removed, either by the collation of manufcripts, or the aid of verfions, internal analogy or external teftimony; the laft refource is conjectural criticifm.—" Conjectural criticifm!" exclaims the fcripture-zealot, " are we then to mend the word of God by conjecture, and fubfti- " tute our own ideas for the dictates of the Holy Ghoft?" Have patience for a moment, and hear at leaft what may be urged in favour of the conjectural critic. Let us firft ftate the queftion as it ought to be. The conjectural critic does not affume the province of *mending the word of God:* his aim is to purify it as much as poſſible from all human admixture: he wiſhes not to ſubſtitute his own ideas for the dictates of the Holy Ghoſt, but to reſtore thoſe dictates to their firſt integrity. His wiſh is certainly pious, and his aim commendable; it remains to be ſeen, how far he is likely to be ſucceſsful.

I ſay then that there are caſes in which the text of an author may be corrected and reſtored by mere critical conjecture; ſometimes with the utmoſt certainty, ſometimes with great appearance of it, and ſometimes only with probability. A few examples from the firſt Engliſh book that comes to hand will put this out of all doubt.

If you ſhould read in ſome faulty copy of Addiſon's firſt dialogue on medals, " Cynthio, Eugenius and Philander had *terited* together " from the town" (which might very eaſily happen from the ſtrong reſemblance in print of the letters *r* and *t*) would you wait for the authority of a manuſcript to reſtore theſe letters to their proper places and read *retired?* Again, if you read, " Their deſign was to " paſs away the heats ſummer," would you heſitate a moment to ſupply the words *of the*, or at leaſt the word *of*, between *heats* and *ſummer?* Once more, if the following words in the ſame dialogue were thus printed, " among the freſh breezes that from riſe the " river," would you deem it any temerity to put *riſe* before *from*, where it evidently ſhould be placed.

In the above examples, the emendations would be all of the utmost certainty. I will now produce some that would be the next thing to certain. Suppose we read, in the same place; " and the " agreeable *ture* of shades and fountains," we must perceive that something is wanting before *ture*, and we shall have little doubt that it is *mix*. Again; " in which the whole country naturally"—*naturally*, what? why, most probably, "abounds:" though, absolutely, it might perhaps be some other synonymous word.

But there are cases where the emendation would be but barely probable, as in the following example : " They were all three well " versed in the politer of learning, and had travelled into the most " nations of Europe." We know some word is wanting after *politer*, but we can only form a probable conjecture what word it is. It is probably *parts*, it may be *branches*; but some such word it must be. It is still harder to say what word should precede *nations*, or whether there is not a word too much in this part of the sentence: for we may fill it up by inserting the word *refined* between *most* and *nations*; or by throwing out the word *the* before *most* : and both emendations would be almost equally probable.

It would be easy to bring similar and still more striking instances from the Latin, Greek and other dead languages; but these, I presume, are more than sufficient to evince, that the text of an author may be corrected, sometimes with certainty, and sometimes with probability, from conjecture alone.

This, indeed, will be readily allowed with regard to other writings; but the BIBLE! the BIBLE! Is the original text of the Bible to be corrected in the same manner? With a proper deference and due diſtinction, I anſwer, undoubtedly it is. If in Ben-chaim's edition of the Hebrew text, for example, one of the commandments had been thus expreſſed; " Thou ſhalt commit adultery," as it is ſaid to have been once printed in an edition of the Engliſh Bible: muſt poſterior editors have waited for manuſcript authority to reſtore the negative particle? Or if, in the example adduced by Houbigant, it were written in our preſent text, through a miſtake not unfrequent with the Maſoretes, " Thou ſhalt adore thy God, and " *not* ſerve him." Muſt that wicked *not* remain there, becauſe we have no manuſcript at hand to correct it by? Surely, ſurely, he muſt be ſcrupulouſly fearful of profaning the Scripture, who would reject an emendation, that reſcues the Scripture itſelf from evident impiety; under pretext, that it is but a conjectural correction *.

* To make this matter ſtill more evident, and to expoſe the abſurdity of thoſe who maintain, that no conjectural emendations of the Hebrew text are admiſſible; let us put the caſe, that our Engliſh Bible were the original Scripture; and that in all the copies of it, whether printed or manuſcript, the ſixth verſe of the ſecond chapter of Ezekiel run thus (as it actually does in an edition I have ſeen:) " Though briars and thorns be with thee, and though " thou deſt *well* among ſcorpions; be not afraid, &c." Let us alſo ſuppoſe that this reading were prior to all tranſlations made from the ſuppoſed original, and could not, conſequently, be rectified by their means; would a critic of the ſmalleſt penetration, ſufficiently acquainted with the grammar and genius of the Engliſh language, and who had maturely conſidered the context and the ſcope of the prophet's words, be at a loſs to perceive, or unwarranted to affirm, that a *d* had been dropt out of the text, and that the original reading muſt have been *dwell?* Or, ſhould he find (as Archbiſhop Secker found in the edition he uſed) in Philip. i.

It is true, however, that all criticism, and particularly sacred criticism, has its due bounds; and nothing is more easy or more common, than to exceed them. A young man of genius and application, who has got a certain tincture of Greek and Hebrew learning; and is able, with the help of a Lexicon, to read his Bible in the original, is but too apt to think he has made wonderful discoveries; and fancies he has hit on the genuine meaning of a thousand obscure passages, that had escaped every prior translator. But if he possess but a small share of good sense, and be not too eager to publish his crude essays, he will soon begin to percieve that he has been precipitate in his march, and will tread the ground over again with a more steady and cautious step. He will not, now, cry out *Euréka* at the first appearance of a discovery, however specious. He will carefully examine it in every point of view, suggest to himself every objection that is likely to be made against it, and adopt it only after mature discussion and full conviction. By proceeding in this manner, he will certainly make fewer discoveries; but those he makes will be more to the purpose. In proportion as he advances in this difficult and dangerous career, he will move with still greater wariness; become every day more diffident

---

16. " to ad dafflicticn to my bonds;" or in Psalm xxxi. 10. " my life is spent with grief and my *ears* with sighing;" or 1 Timothy i. 2. Grace, mercy, peace from God our Father and Jesus Christ *of* Lord;" would he be rash in conjecturing that *of* should be *ear ; ears, years ;* and *ad daffliction, add affliction?* I hardly think that any one in his right senses, would find fault with such emendations; though made without the authority of either manuscript or version.

of his critical acumen; doubt of many of his former affumptions; often find himfelf conftrained to admit as highly plaufible, what he had once rejected as abfurd; and be contented with offering an opinion, where he had before uttered a decifion. Such is the procedure of the fage and fober critic, whether he has to correct his text, or to explain it when corrected.

To give a minute detail of all the rules, and exceptions from the rules, that ought to guide him as he goes along, and which he never ought to lofe fight of, would alone make a volume as large as Defpauter. But they are all ultimately reducible to the four following general and comprehenfive canons, the ufe of which is not limited to conjectural criticifm only; but extends to every other fource of emendation.

The firft canon is, never to fuppofe that the text is corrupted, without the moft cogent and convincing reafons. For if, as the judicious Rollin remarks, when altering the text of any author is in queftion, one muft be, as it were, compelled to it by a fort of abfolute neceffity, and have almoft an evidence of the corruption; how much more ftrictly is this rule to be obferved, with regard to the text of Scripture?

The fecond canon is, never to have recourfe to conjectural criticifm, until every other fource has been tried and exhaufted; for it would be ridiculous to exert even the greateft ingenuity, in gueffing, when we may attain our end, by readier and lefs deceptious means.

The third—Let all corrections be confiftent with the text and with one another; that is to fay, let there be nothing in the correction that does not perfectly agree with what precedes and follows, and that is not fupported by grammatical analogy.

The fourth—Infert no correction, however plaufible or even certain, in the text, without warning the reader, and diftinguifhing it by a proper note.

Thefe canons ftrictly adhered to, and difcreetly ufed, we fee no danger in correcting the Hebrew text. Nay, until it be thus corrected, we fhall never have a good tranflation of it.

But the corruptions of the prefent text are not the fole difficulty the tranflator has to furmount. To afcertain the true meaning is often as hard as to afcertain the true reading; and this has been another great caufe of the imperfection of modern tranflations: a caufe which, perhaps, will never be wholly removed.

There is no language fo compleatly copious and diftinctive as to have a different *vocable* for every different idea. Our own, after all the refinement it has received, is wonderfully defective in this refpect; and we yet want a great number of terms to exprefs the vaft variety of our conceptions. Hence it requires no fmall fkill in the art of writing, to avoid, at all times, equivocation or amphibology.

But this is much more fenfibly perceived in the Hebrew than, perhaps, any other language. The paucity of its compounds, the uncertainty of its derivations, the frequent coincidences and confimilarities of its inflexions, an almost total want of abstracts and modifiers, the many and multifarious significations of the same particle—these and other similar obstacles impede the translator's progress at every step, and oblige him to grope his way with great caution and diffidence.

Besides, even the radical signification of many words is extremely uncertain: nor needs this at all to surprize us. If there are terms and phrases in Shakespeare, who wrote in our own language and touched almost on our own days, already become unintelligible to our best glossarists; how difficult must it be to decypher the words of a language, that has ceased to be a living one for two thousand years; is all contained in one not bulky volume; and of which several words and modes of expression occur but seldom, or only once?

Add to these the difficulties that arise from the great diversity of stile in the different Hebrew writers, from references to monuments that no more exist; from frequent allusions to facts that are not recorded or but barely hinted; from proverbial sayings, poetical licences, uncommonly bold metaphors, and obscure allegories: not to mention the very great difference of laws, manners and local usages; which are well known to have great influence on the language of a nation, and must have particularly affected that of the Jews, who, in those respects, so widely differed from all other nations. Whoever considers all this duly, will be convinced, even without the light of experience, that the route of the Bible-tranflator is neither fmooth nor even; and that it behoves him to walk in it with the utmoft warinefs.

It may, neverthelefs, be confidently affirmed, that the greateft part of thofe who have entered into it for thefe laft three hundred years, have voluntarily put out their own eyes, and allowed themfelves to be led on by the worft of guides. The fame impofing fet of men, who had the audacity and art to make the Chriftian world believe that they had preferved the text of their Scriptures in its original integrity, by a pretended enumeration of every word and letter, found it equally eafy to perfwade them, that the true reading and meaning had alfo been preferved by the punctuation of every fyllable, and the diftinction of every paufe. This was a fecond part of that wonderful MASORA, without which the Hebrew text was fuppofed to be a mere dead letter, a nofe of wax, a body without a foul *.

I will not here engage in the much agitated controverfy about the antiquity and authority of the vowel points. Capellus, Mafclef, Houbigant and Sharp have nearly exhaufted the fubject; and the efforts, that have been made to refute their arguments, have only fhewn more clearly how invincible they are. The vowel points, whether they be the fruit of the fifth or of the tenth century, are certainly a rabbinical, and, in many refpects, but a pue-

* *Nafum cereum, corpus expers animae.* Guarin. praefat. in Gram. Heb.

rile production *. Confidered, indeed, as a mere human work they may be allowed to have fome little utility. They fhew us how the Hebrew was pronounced at the time of their invention.

* To give the reader, who is not acquainted with Hebrew grammar, fome, not unfavourable, idea of Maforetic punctuation, let us fuppofe that the prefent Englifh verfion of the Bible were the original; and written, as the original formerly was, in one uniform character, and without any of our modern marks of diftinction. In this fuppofition, the text would run thus:

INTHEBEGINNINGGODCREAT EDTHEHEAUENANDTHEEARTH

Let us next fuppofe that fome ingenious pedagogue, remarking the great difference between this orthography and the prefent orthöepy; and obferving, alfo, that fo clofe and connected an arrangement of words and letters is attended with fome difficulty to unpractifed readers; fhould fet himfelf to contrive expedients; to remove thofe inconveniences; and, for that purpofe, fhould reafon in the following manner: " Our alphabet has but five vowels to " exprefs fifteen vocal founds;—Some of our confonants vary their powers according to their " fituation; and fome of them have occafionally no power at all. The fame letter is fome-" times an afpirate and fometimes not. Many words have more than one fignification with " out any difference in the mode of utterance. Our written language has no paufal marks, " and our profody is not regulated by any tonic diftinctions. To remedy thefe evils, and to " fix the true Englifh pronunciation for all time to come, let our fifteen vowel founds be re-" prefented by as many different fymbols.

" A open by		E fhort by		O long by	
" A clofe by		E obfcure by		O fhort by	
" A broad by		I long by		U long by	
" A flender by		I fhort by		U fhort by	
" E long by		I French by		U Englifh	

" Then, let the hard founds of C and G, I and V confonants, and all quiefcents be marked " with a dot above, and the afpirate H and hiffing S with a fmall horizontal line.—Let all " words be feparated by proper fpaces, and diftinguifhed by proportionate paufes. Let

* The fymbols of I fhort, O long, and U long, are the fame; but the firft is placed below the line, the fecond above, and the laft in the middle.

They diftinguifh, although not always juftly, the different accep‐
tations of the fame or nearly fimilar words. In our prefent faulty
text, they often fupply the want of many formative letters; and,

" A full paufe be marked thus |
" A fmaller paufe thus   ʌ   } both below the line.
" A ftill fmaller paufe thus   :
" And the fmalleft of all thus   ׃׃ } both above the line."

He faid, and ftraightway fell to work: and lo! the whole Bible, in his induftrious hands,
affumed in due time this rare appearance,

IN THE BEGINNING GOD CREA
TED THE HEAUEN AND THE EARTH

It is of no importance, whether thefe fymbols, which are indeed the very rabbinical points,
are as accurately combined, and adapted to our language, as they might be: they are fuffi‐
ciently fo to exprefs the idea that is meant to be conveyed; and now, my good reader, what
think you of this improvement? " The diftinction of words, you will fay, is well enough: the
" marks of paufation, though multiplied without neceffity, may alfo have their ufe: but to
" attempt to fix a pronunciation that is ever fluctuating, and tones that are continually
" changing, by any other rules than the prefent ufage, and the practice of the beft fpeakers,
" is a foolifh and fruitlefs attempt. For how are the powers of thefe very fymbols afcertain‐
" ed, but by an immediate appeal to living founds and the now prevailing modes of utterance?
" If thefe happen to change, as we know they imperceptibly do, what will be the ufe of your
" boafted fymbols at any future period? and by what canons will their refpective powers be
" afcertained? Granting even, that they had, like Ezekiel's myftic wheels, a living and felf-in‐
" terpretating fpirit within them, that could effectually and for ever arreft fo fleeting a thing
" as vocal air; why is their pofition in the text fo awkward and unnatural? Why are they ge‐
" nerally placed, not beneath the vowels, the various powers of which they are fuppofed
" to denote, but beneath the preceding or following confonant?" Stop, my honeft friend;
you are now quite miftaken: there are, no more, any vowels in the Englifh alphabet.
" What? *a, e, i, o, u*, not vowels?" By no means: they are all confonants; mute confonants!—
Have you any thing more to object?—" I have: Such a motley multitude of pricks and points

I

thereby, serve to more readily discriminate genders, numbers, persons, moods and tenses; although here, too, the discrimination is often arbitrary and sometimes manifestly wrong. In short, they are a kind of grammatical comment on the text; and, if they had never been pushed forward in any other light, they might have been permitted to hold a subordinate rank among works of the same nature: but to impose them upon us as of divine authority, was the height of impudence, and to receive them as such the height of credulity.

As such, however, they were generally received by almost all

"disfigure the beauty and symmetry of the text, and often confuse the mind, as much as they bewilder the eye; and I dislike every thing that produceth confusion." Good! But what if our pedagogue had crowded the scene with a whole host more of *regal* and *ministerial* attendants (for so the Hebrew grammarians denominate their accents) with *sakeph-katons* and *sakeph-gadols; pashtas* and *karneparas; shalshaleths* and *mercakephalas*, and twenty other such barbarous names; of which, although it requires a little code of laws to marshal them, and although Bohlius is said to have in vain employed seven long years for that laudable purpose, yet neither he nor any one else could ever point out the uses? What, if instead of the true English pronunciation, he had given you a Scotch or Irish one? What if even his division of words and sentences were often not only trifling but palpably erroneous? What if other pedagogues, improving on his improvements, had thrown out, by degrees, the original vowels, now become useless lumber; and if instead of GOD, HEAVEN, EARTH, you were presented with GD, HVN, ERTH, bespattered with pricks and patches as above? What if such elisions were called natural anomalies of English grammar? What—" Sweep all that trash away," you would undoubtedly exclaim, "and give me again the plain old unpointed text of my Bible."

Such trash is the greatest part of the Masoretic points, which rabbinical pedagogues would impose upon us as the only sure interpreter of the Hebrew scripture! Whoever wishes to see, to what degree of absurdity, or insanity, even Christian writers have been led by this imposition, may read Wasmuth's *Institutions;* Ousel *de accentuatione Hebraica;* or Walter Cross's *Taghmical art*, published at London in the year 1698.

Proteſtant communions *, from this ridiculous notion, that if they were once allowed to be a human invention, the infallibility of the Scripture, as a rule of faith, would be precarious; and the fundamental article of Proteſtantiſm be overturned at one blow. This blow, neverthelefs, a Proteſtant divine † was not afraid to ſtrike; and he ſtruck it ſo effectually, that all the rabbinical learning and dialectical ſkill of the Buxtorfs were not able to ward it.

But what could not be done by ſkill or learning, was done by dint of authority. In the year 1679 a ſpecial canon was framed at Geneva and adopted by all the Helvetian churches; by which it was decreed that no one ſhould in future be admitted to the ſacred miniſtry, who did not publicly acknowledge the Maſoretic text to be divine and authentic; both as to *conſonants*‡ and *vowels*. They had only one ſtep further to go; and that was, to decree the myſteries of the *Cabbala* to be of divine origin.

Although the Geneva canon, backed by reams of annual theſes from the Dutch univerſities, ſuſpended for a while the fate of the

---

* This is the more remarkable, as the firſt Reformers and their diſciples, for nearly a century, were of a very different opinion (ſee Hody *de text. original.* p. 553.) But there is a cauſe for every thing. The diſpute about the *Judge* of controverſies had been warmly agitated between them and the Catholic party; and they thought they could not better anſwer ſome troubleſome objections of the latter, than by maintaining that the vowel points were of divine origin. What is ſtill more ſtrange, there were ſome few Catholics of the ſame opinion. Even Arias Montanus leans that way; and Poſtellus went further than ever did Jew or Proteſtant: he affirmed that God himſelf had made a preſent of the *Maſora* to Adam.

† Louis Cappel a French Calviniſt and profeſſor of the Hebrew at Saumur.

‡ In the language of that time, all the letters of the Hebrew alphabet were called conſonants.

Maforetic Dagon, it could not long prevent its downfal. The moſt learned of all countries were generally on the ſide of Capellus; and their auxiliary attacks were the more fuccefsful, as fome of them were deſerters from the other party and knew its weakeſt holds. Still fome feeble efforts were made, from time to time, to ſupport the tottering idol: but he now ſeems to lie proſtrate on the threſhold of his own temple, never, we apprehend, to be raiſed again*.

But if we reject the Maforetic points and accents, what ſhall we fubſtitute in their place? Muſt we diveſt the text of every thing but the bare elements, and divide and explain it as we pleaſe? Not as we pleaſe but as we ought, and in the ſame manner we ſhould divide and explain any other author. The firſt part of this taſk will indeed be eaſy, if we have accompliſhed the latter. The true meaning once aſcertained, the neceſſary diviſions will readily preſent themſelves: nor is it material whether they be always the moſt proper that might be found, or not. It is fufficient that they cre-

* The laſt publication in this country in favour of the Maforetic ſyſtem is, I believe, the ſecond edition of a Hebrew grammar, in Latin, by Dr. James Robertſon, profeſſor of the oriental languages in the Univerſity of Edinburgh; printed there in 1783. In the preface, notes and appendix to this work, the learned profeſſor has collected from the Buxtorfs, Leufden, Schultens, Guarin, the French encyclopediſts, Memoires de literature, &c. the moſt plauſible arguments that have been urged by the punctuiſts ſince the beginning of the controverſy. The appendix and part of the notes are chiefly intended to combat the oppoſite ſyſtem as adopted and defended by profeſſor Wilſon of the Univerſity of St. Andrews; who had, the year before, publiſhed, for the uſe of his own claſs, *Elements of Hebrew Grammar;* which, conſidered as an elementary book, wants nothing to recommend it to the public but a better Hebrew type. His antagoniſt has been far more fortunate in his printer.

ate no embarrassment or confusion, by disjoining what ought to be connected; or by connecting what ought to be disjoined, as the Masoretic divisions not seldom do *.

The great object, then, is to come at the true signification of every word and sentence; and this, I affirm from experience, we shall better accomplish with an unpointed text before us, than with a pointed one: especially if, in the latter case, we sit down to translate, prepossessed with an idea, that the points are to be our only guides.

I say, "only guides:" for I would not exclude them from the translator's notice. They may occasionally be consulted, not as

---

* This, indeed, ought to be reckoned among the causes of the imperfection of modern versions. For there is hardly a modern translator, who has not, more or less, been led astray by the present division and punctuation of the Hebrew text; even when the text itself is sufficiently clear and obvious, to make any deviation from it unexcusable. The division of the chapters is often improper, but that of the verses is infinitely more so. We are in many places presented with a full periodical distinction, where there should not be so much as the smallest pause; nominatives are separated from their verbs, adjectives from their substantives, and even letters and syllables are cruelly divorced from the words they naturally belong to. "Nothing," says a sensible writer in the Critical Review (vol. xviii. p. 188.) "has been more injurious to the sa" cred writings, than the common method of dividing them into chapters and verses; by which " means the chain of reasoning is frequently broken, the sentences mangled, the eye misguid" ed, the attention bewildered, and the meaning lost." This is, indeed, high colouring; but still the likeness is true: and there are many instances, both in the Old and New Testament, of mistakes and mistranslations from this cause. Absurd as the present divisions often are, there is yet an almost absolute necessity of retaining them, in some shape or other. According to them our Concordances and Indexes have been formed; and references and quotations made for two hundred years back; it would therefore create much confusion to remove such land-marks. But we may remove the evils which they have caused.

oracles, but as opinions; which we may adopt, or reject, as we judge it expedient: but, I believe, we shall rarely, by their assistance, overcome a real difficulty, which we could not have overcome without it. Even their greatest pretended utility, that of supplying a number of servile letters which are wanting in our printed Hebrew Bibles, is in a great measure superseded by the collation of manuscripts; in which we luckily find those very letters, which the punctuists would have us ridiculously believe, were originally wanting in the autographs; although the want of them leaves such grammatical irregularities in the text, as no written language ever acknowledged.

And here I cannot help remarking, that the Masoretic punctuation has been productive of the greatest evil, where it has been credulously supposed to be the most productive of good. The real vocal letters, being once stript of their vocal powers and deemed quiescent consonants, were gradually thrown out as useless, or omitted as unnecessary; according to the negligence or caprice of transcribers: for what need is there (they probably said) scrupulously to retain a *vau*, when a *holem* or *kibbutz* performs its functions; or a *jod* when its place is so well supplied by a *hirik-katon*, *tzere* or *segol?** Hence we do not meet with any two manuscripts,

---

* The *jod* and *vau* are important Hebrew formatives. The first is the characteristic of the masculine plural of nouns and of the transitive voice of verbs, not to mention other purposes which it formerly seems to have served; the *vau* is the characteristic of feminine plurals and

that are alike in thefe particulars; and by far the greateſt number of various readings arife from the accidental or intentional omiſſion of thofe two letters.

But if the *Maſora* is confidered as an unfure and infufficient guide, to lead us to the true meaning of the Hebrew fcriptures, what other methods fhall we take to attain our end? The very fame we take to underftand the Greek and Latin authors. We muſt, firſt of all, learn the grammar and vocabulary of the language; we muſt ſtudy its peculiar ſtructure and genius; obferve its fingularities, anomalies, and analogy with other tongues; confult the beft lexicons, concordances * and grammatical commentaries; confider attentively the fcope, ftile and phrafeology of every

---

of two of the participles: but in all thefe refpects they are both wanting, in an infinite number of places, in the prefent printed text; and this want is urged by punctuifts as a proof of the utility, not to fay neceffity, of the vowel-points. Ye are in the right, Gentlemen! When ye have undermined a building by taking away fome of its chief fupports, ye muſt ſtay it with fuch materials as ye have; and ye may then infift on their being neceffary: but if we can by any means replace the original ftone pillars, we fhall have no further ufe for your wooden props.

* Of all the helps towards underftanding the Hebrew fcriptures a good concordance is undoubtedly the moft ufeful. But we yet want a good concordance; and the man who fhould devote five or fix years to the compiling of one from Buxtorf, Calafio, Noldius, Taylor, Kircher, Montfaucon and Trommius, would do a fingular fervice to Biblical ftudents. Buxtorf's method of arrangement, with very little improvement, fhould be ftrictly followed; the errors of orthography rectified from the authority of manufcripts and other fources of emendation; and the various acceptations of the fame word in the ancient verfions exactly noted and methodically diftinguifhed. Such a work would be worth all the commentaries that ever have been made.

different writer; carefully diftinguifh the natural from the figurative, poetical from profaic compofition; compare author with author, paffage with paffage, image with image, trope with trope; fo as that all the parts of the whole text may mutually throw light on one another:—and, becaufe the whole text together makes but an ordinary volume, and contains many words and phrafes, that occur but once or extremely feldom, we muft, for the better underftanding of thefe, call into our aid the other Oriental kindred dialects; the Chaldee, Syriac, Samaritan, Ethiopic and Arabic. The three firft have fo great an affinity of idiom with the Hebrew, that they may be confidered as coufin-germans of the fame family; and though the other two are not quite fo near a-kin, their relationfhip is not lefs evident *. From all of them, therefore, may be derived helps towards inveftigating the radical fignification of obfcure words, and illuftrating modes of expreffion that would, elfe, be inexplicable. A comparative dictionary of all thofe dialects would be a moft ufeful work. With half the bulk of Caftel's, it might be made much more copious and correct; and, to render the analogy more ftriking, it fhould, I think, be all in the Hebrew character, like Schindler's pentaglott lexicon. Such a

---

* The Arabic has one advantage which the other dialects do not, in the fame degree, poffefs. It is ftill a living language, the moft extenfively fpoken, and, in fome refpects, the moft copious of all languages. There are extant in it a great many elegant compofitions on all forts of fubjects, both in profe and poetry; and the ftudy of it has, of late years, been greatly promoted by fome of the moft learned men of the age.

work I have long had in contemplation*: but alas! *Iter longum, brevis aetas:* We may grasp at immensity in idea; but our span is, in reality, the span of a pigmy.

Until some literary drudge be found, with patience and sufficient leisure to go through so tedious a labour, we must be content with picking from Buxtorf, Schaaf, Crinesius, Ludolf, Mininski, Golius and Richardson, such information as we can get; though we shall be frequently disappointed, and obliged to confess, that the succours, we draw from such sources, are but small, in proportion to the pains they cost us. Etymological conjectures are of all the most fallacious; and it requires much penetration, a nice discerning taste, and a long and serious ponderation of circumstances, to be able, amidst a number of almost equally probable derivations, to determine which is likeliest to be the true one. When we have toiled, for example, through Schultens's tedious and disgusting book of *Hebrew origins*, we have only learned, how little we can learn from such sort of discussions; and are vexed that we spent so much time to so little purpose.

Our next great resources, therefore, after a long analytical and comparative study of the Hebrew language itself, are the ancient versions; which not only afford the best helps for correcting the

---

* As a proper introduction to such a work, I formed, many years ago, the plan of a *Comparative Grammar of the principal Oriental dialects;* which, by way of relaxation from more serious studies, I am now compleating, and preparing for the press—not doubting but the smallest attempt to facilitate the study of those languages, and thereby to promote Biblical knowledge, will be favourably received by the serious part of the public.

text; but are also, in general, the best interpreters of its genuine meaning. I will not say, with Vossius, that, if we had not those versions, particularly that of the Septuagint, we should be able to make no translation at all; but I think it may be confidently affirmed that a translation, made without their aid, would, in many places, be extremely imperfect and uncertain; and that it has happened, by a most singular providence, that they have been transmitted to us in so many different forms; as if for that very purpose. Yet we are not implicitly to follow them, any more than the *Masora*. We are ever to remember that they likewise have their faults and corruptions; and that nearly the same precautions are necessary, when we consult them as interpreters; as when we employ them as *correctoria*. What has been already said of them, in the one respect, is applicable in the other.

Neither are we to neglect the modern versions, whether Latin or vernacular, that have been made since the revival of letters. For although they are almost all made from the present Masoretic text, and consequently participate of all its defects; there are few of them from which a diligent and judicious translator may not draw some advantage: let us here take a short review of them; beginning by those in Latin.

The most ancient *, and, in a great measure, the model of all

---

* I omit mentioning, such modern Latin translations as are only in manuscript, several of which are said to be extant in different libraries; as also such party-coloured versions as those of Osiander, Clarius, &c, which are only interpolated editions of the Latin Vulgate.

the reſt, was that of Santes Pagninus, printed firſt at Florence in the year 1528. It was the work of twenty five years, and has been greatly extolled both by Jews and Chriſtians, as the beſt Latin verſion that ever was made from the Hebrew; that of Jerom not excepted. It is, for all that, a barbarous compoſition, deſpicable in almoſt every point of view, but that of a grammatical gloſſary: as ſuch it may be of conſiderable uſe in giving an idea of the Hebrew idiom, and a ſuperficial knowledge of the language to grown up Biblical ſtudents, who are too idle to turn over the leaves of a lexicon, or con their Buxtorf. It was made yet more horridly uncouth by Arias Montanus, who interlined it in his edition of the Hebrew text of the Antwerp polyglott, from which it unaccountably found its way into that of London.

Next, in priority of time, is the verſion of Munſter, which appeared about the year 1534. It is little leſs literal, but more perſpicuous and elegant than that of Pagninus. The rabbins were his chief guides; and his annotations are compiled with no ſmall diſcernment from their beſt works.

Of a ſtill purer Latinity and greater perſpicuity is the tranſlation of Leo-Juda, commonly called the Tigurine Bible; becauſe it was publiſhed by the divines of Zurich. The firſt edition is of 1543. It has been ſince frequently republiſhed in different kingdoms; and with ſome ſmall alterations, even by the Catholic Univerſity of Salamanca, in 1584.

Hitherto the new translators of the Bible had moved nearly in the same track; all pursuing, with more or less attention and fidelity, the route which the rabbins had marked out for them; and making the Masora the pole-star by which they steered. Castalio had the courage to strike out a path for himself. He translated, indeed, from the present Hebrew text, but he did not Judaically despise the ancient versions. The principal, and often necessary, supplements which are found in them, but wanting in the Masoretic copies, he inserted with proper distinctions *: nor did he reject those useful and excellent books, which most Protestants have, after St. Jerom and his Hebrew preceptors, too rashly thrown out of the canon and branded with the name of *Apocrypha*; but which, in the most ancient copies of the Greek, Syriac and Latin versions, are intermixed and rank with the other books: and, to connect the Old Testament with the New, he inserted two excellent supplements, abridged from Josephus; the one after the fourth book of Esdras, and the other at the end of the Machabees.

Castalio deviated no less from his predecessors in his mode of translating. They had crept, like timid and ignoble slaves, after an imperious master; he claimed the privilege of walking side by side. His version is bold and free, his stile clear and concise, his diction pure and perhaps scrupulously elegant. It was reprobated,

---

* To additions from the Greek he prefixed a G; to those from the Latin an L; when from both, G. L. An H denoted the end of the addition.

however, in general by Jews and Christians, by Catholics and Protestants, as a temerarious, insolent and even impious burlesque of Holy writ. The theologians of Geneva, with Beza at their head, were particularly harsh in their censures of it. But more cool and candid estimators have given a very different judgment. Simler, Huetius, Buxtorf, Duport, and, above all, Episcopius have borne honourable testimony in its favour; and whoever reads it without prepossession, and compares it carefully with the originals, will, we doubt not, be of the opinion of Dr. Mead, that it is not only a most elegant but also a most faithful version*. Had the author worked upon a better text, retained a little more of the idiomatical simplicity of his originals, and been somewhat less lavish of his oratorial graces and classical refinements, his translation would, altogether, be the first of modern times. As it is, I make no hesitation to give it as my opinion, that a more compleat, more impartial or more faithful version will not easily be found. The best edition is that of Basil, in folio, in 1573.

About two years after, was published a new Latin version of the Old Testament, by Junius and Tremellius; to which, in the second and all posterior editions, was added Beza's translation of the New Testament. It has been often retouched and reprinted, both in

---

* Quam, habita multis in locis collatione, non modo Latinissimam, sed etiam accuratissimam et ad sensum mentemque dictorum, tam in Hebraeis quam in Graecis, maximè accomodatam deprehendi. Praefat. in Medicam. Sacr.

Germany and in England; and was long in high eſtimation among Maſoretic Proteſtants: yet it never entirely recovered from the diſcredit thrown upon it by Druſius, and is now almoſt ſunk into oblivion. It muſt be confeſſed, however, that it merited a better fate: and although it deſerves not the exceſſive eulogiums of Poole, it is neither ſo unfaithful nor ſo arbitrary as ſome critics pretend. The reproach of its being a paraphraſe rather than a tranſlation, is the worſt founded of all reproaches. It often runs into the other extreme, and is, in ſome reſpects, more ſervile than that of Pagninus. To me its chief defects appear to be an impure and barbarous Latinity, an affected mode of conſtruction, and a ſtrange disfigurement of the Hebrew names, to make them agreeable to the Maſoretic punctuation.

The famous Cardinal de Vio Cajetan, who, amidſt a multiplicity of ſtate affairs, found means to devote a part of every day to ſerious ſtudy, left behind him, among other laborious productions, a tranſlation of a great part of the Bible. As he was totally ignorant of the Hebrew, he employed two learned Rabbins, a Jew and a Chriſtian, as his interpreters; and having a ſound judgement and diſcerning taſte, he ſucceeded much better than could be expected. But his verſion was formed on this erroneous principle, that a tranſlation of the Scripture cannot be too literal; ſhould it even, for that reaſon, be unintelligible. This prepoſſeſſion made him judge unfavorably of the Vulgate; which he often cenſures without reason: for which cause some zealots have unjustly taxed him with heresy. His translation has much the same faults with that of Pagninus; and may be of much the same use to the Hebrew student. It was printed, with his commentary, at Lyons in the year 1639.

At the same place, in 1650, was published another Latin version of the Bible, as far as Ezekiel, with a tedious commentary, by Malvenda, a Spanish Dominican. He did well to add a commentary; for, without it, his translation would be often perfectly unintelligible: so barbarous is his stile, and so unhappy his choice of expressions. " If any one, says F. Simon, wishes to have a transla-" tion of the Scriptures purely grammatical, let him use that of " Malvenda." I should rather say, is any one madly fond of a version servilely literal? Let him read Malvenda's; and I shall wonder much, if he be not soon cured of his phrenzy.

A new Latin version of the whole Bible, by Sebastian Schmidt, was published at Strasburg in the year 1696. It is said to have been on the anvil near forty years, and is evidently, laboured with great care and pains. It is clear, concise and not inelegant; and if the author had been possest of a better text, and had paid some more attention to the ancient versions, his work would have been a valuable accession to the Biblical library. A more correct edition of it was given by the divines of Strasburg, in the year 1708: and it has been since republished, in Germany, along with the Hebrew text.

PROSPECTUS.

John Le Clerc, profeſſor of philoſophy, belles lettres and Hebrew in the college of the Remonſtrants at Amſterdam, and one of the moſt univerſal ſcholars of his time, publiſhed a new Latin verſion of the Pentateuch in 1710. The reſt of his tranſlation, which comprehends the greateſt part of the Holy Scriptures, appeared at different periods and places; and a compleat edition of the whole was printed at Amſterdam in 1731. Though this verſion has little in it to claim a diſtinguiſhed ſuperiority over thoſe that preceded, it does not deſerve the contempt, with which it is treated by Houbigant, who ſeems to have inherited all Simon's prepoſſeſſions againſt the author, and omits no opportunity of depretiating his labours. Had Le Clerc lived in our days, and been convinced of the neceſſity of correcting the text, before he attempted to tranſlate it, he was certainly capable of producing a much better work; eſpecially if he had learnt to write with a little more difficulty, and kept the *operoſa carmina fingo* of Horace always in mind. But he wrote in too great a hurry, and on too many ſubjects, to write excellently on any ſubject; and, although extremely confident of his own abilities and bold in his aſſertions, yet was unaccountably, more or leſs, a ſlave to rabbinical prejudices.

To ſhake of theſe entirely, and to open a new and rational career to the Biblical critic, was reſerved for Houbigant. That truly learned man, who died only in 1783, in the ninety eighth year of his age, had early applied to the ſtudy of the Oriental languages, in a fociety where they have long been cultivated with great fuccefs. Having learned the Hebrew according to Mafclef's new method, and compiled an excellent little dictionary, on the fame principles, under the title of *Racines Hebraiques fans points-voyelles*, he formed the plan of a new verfion of the Old Teftament; not from the prefent printed Maforetic copies, which Capellus and others had fo invincibly proved to be erroneous; but from a copy corrected by fuch means, and from fuch fources of emendation, as he conceived the moft likely to anfwer the purpofe; and which are, in general, the fame that have been fpecified in the former part of this Profpectus. With what ingenuity and judgment he has executed the great defign, is well known to thofe who have perufed his work. Nothing can exceed the purity, fimplicity, perfpicuity and energy of his tranflation; and if he has not always been equally happy in his conjectural emendation of the text, it cannot be denied that he has, at leaft, carried away the palm from all thofe who preceded him in the fame career. The clamors that have been raifed againft him are the clamors of illiberal ignorance, or of partiality to a fyftem which he had turned into ridicule. While his mode of interpreting is approved and imitated by a Lowth, a Kennicott, a Michaelis and a Starck, the barkings of inferior critics will not much injure him. Houbigant's verfion, accompanied with the Hebrew text of Vanderhooght, *prolegomena* and critical notes, was publifhed in the moft fplendid manner at Paris, between

L

the years 1747 and 1753, in four folio volumes; and is already become a rare and coftly book *.

Befides thofe general Latin verfions, we have a great many others of fome particular books or parts of books, by Zuinglius, Oecolampadius, Melanchton, Drufius, Pifcator, Mufculus, Mafius, Terfer, Brentius, Bolducius, Juftiniani, Felix Pratenfis, Pellicanus, Genebrard, De-Muis, Ferrandus, Cocceius, Leufden, &c. of all which the induftrious tranflator will avail himfelf, as far as he has it in his power; and from all which he may actually gather fome grains of fterling ore.

What has been faid of modern Latin, is equally applicable to modern vernacular tranflations. They are all caft, as it were, in the fame mould; all fcrupuloufly literal verfions of the fame faulty originals, and, almoft always, under the guidance of Pagninus. The moft diftinguifhing characters of thofe we are acquainted with fhall be given in very few words.

The firft vernacular verfion made in Europe from the originals, is the German of Luther. It was publifhed, in parts, between the years 1522 and 1533; and, for the firft time, all together in 1535. Since that time it has been often reprinted, with various corrections and interpolations, to adapt it to the different communions in Germany; and even tranflated, as an architype, into other Teutonic

---

* The verfion was publifhed feparately in feven volumes large octavo; and there is a third edition of the Pfalms in twelves, along with the Vulgate, of the year 1755.

dialects. It is certainly a wonderful production. If it be confidered in what turbulent times, and amidft what variety of other avocations it was made, we are at a lofs to comprehend how one man, who had no model to follow, (for Ulenberg's barbarous verfion from the Vulgate cannot be fo called) could, in fo fhort a fpace and with fuch fcanty helps, accomplifh fo great a work. The Catholics and Calvinifts have often decried it without reafon; and more, perhaps, out of odium to its author than from a regard for truth. There are, indeed, fome paffages in the firft editions, which he feems to have wrefted a little, to make them fpeak more explicitly his favorite tenet of juftification by faith alone. But thefe were few in number, and were rectified in pofterior editions. That of the year 1542 was carefully revifed by himfelf, with the affiftance of fome of the moft learned men of that age; * and again juft before his death in 1545.

Although the language of Luther's verfion had already in 1684 become fo obfolete, that a gloffary was found neceffary for underftanding it; and although it may be eafily fuppofed, that a century more, in the prefent progrefs of the German tongue, has given it a ftill more antique mien; yet it retains, in a great meafure, its firft celebrity; and has not only triumphed over all former at-

* Melanchton, Julus Jonas, Cruciger, Bugenhafius, Zeigler, Forftenius, Rorarius. By thefe it was collated not only with the Hebrew text, but alfo with the Chaldee paraphrafes and the Greek and Latin verfions: for we have already obferved that the abfurd idea of Maforetic infallibility had not yet been adopted by the reformers.

tempts to supersede it, but is, at this day, preferred by many Germans to their latteſt versions.

This, however, cannot, I think, be long the caſe: for if any man be equal to a good tranſlation of the Bible, it is ſurely Michaelis. His erudition, taſte and judgment are well known in the literary world by his numerous and various productions; and his verſion of the Old Teſtament, which is now happily concluded, muſt appear to thoſe, who can reliſh all its beauties, one of the beſt that ever was made. He has, I know, been blamed for deviating too widely from the letter of his text. But his apology is obvious: he tranſlated to be underſtood; and if he cannot be convicted of having miſtaken or miſrepreſented the meaning of his author, he cannot ſurely be, with juſtice, cenſured for conſulting the pleaſure and profit of his reader. But it is impoſſible to pleaſe ſome critics, becauſe they will not be pleaſed. Michaelis is not a blind admirer of the Maſora, and cannot be brooked by thoſe who are.

The Belgic and other northern churches had, for ſome time, no other verſion of the Scripture, but that of Luther; tranſlated into their reſpective tongues, and altered, from time to time, by every new editor. But the States General of Holland, in conſequence of a decree of the Synod of Dort, ordered a new Dutch tranſlation to be made from the originals; which was publiſhed in the year 1636. A particular account of it may be read in Leuſden [*], who gives it much more than due praiſe.

[*] Philol. Hebr. mixt. diſſert. xi.

In like manner, a new Danish version, by Refenius Bishop of Seelandt, was published by the authority of Christian IV. in 1607. But the Swedes, I believe, have yet no other translation than that from Luther's, again and again corrected by different hands.*.

The French translation, published at Neufchâtel in the year 1535, was the hasty production of Olivetan, assisted by Calvin; but it was, afterwards, so often revised and patched by different persons, that it scarcely retains any part of its first texture. After all, it is but an indifferent version, and very far from that perfection which might have been expected from the labours of such learned men as Bertram, Beza, Jaquemot, Goulart, Marez, Martin, &c. Some particular passages, however, I have found better rendered in it, than in any other Masoretic version.

Another French translation, by Diodati, was published at Geneva in 1644, and was well received by the Calvinists. It is not so literal as that of Olivetan, but much more elegant and perspicuous; which is the more to be wondered at, as the author was an Italian, and the same person who had, some years before, given a most elegant Italian translation; of which, in the sequel.

In fine, Le Cene's version, after a new plan of his own, appeared in 1707, but did not meet with the reception he expected. His *Projét*, which was translated into English by Hugh Ross, and

---

* I am informed by Mr. Woide that a new Swedish version of the Bible has been lately made; and that it is a very good one.

basely published as an original work, contains many good observations, and some excellent rules for translating well: but to these he seems not to have always paid due attention himself; and his translation may be said, like Pope's woman, to have no uniform character at all. He is, sometimes, too scrupulously literal; and, sometimes, too free a paraphrast. His stile is incorrect, his diction impure, his expressions often trite and ill-chosen, and as often affectedly *neoterical*. It must, however, be allowed, that he has more frequently hit on the true meaning of his original, than any French translator that went before him; that he is never, or rarely, obscure; and that he is very seldom biassed by party prejudices.

Since Le Cene's version, several particular parts of the Bible have either been newly translated, or improved on the Geneva version, by Le Clerc, Saurin, Beausobre, Chais and other French Calvinists in Holland.

Bruccioli's Italian version from the originals, or rather from the Latin of Pagninus, was first published at Venice in 1532; but the best edition is that of Zanetti in 1540. This version was interpolated, and adapted to the Vulgate, by Marmochini; whose edition, dedicated to the Bishop of Rodez, appeared in 1538. It was also corrected and improved by Rusticius, and published at Geneva in 1562. With all these pretended alterations, corrections and improvements, it is still but a poor translation, compared with that of Diodati, which was first published at Geneva in 1607. There is an elegance and ease in this translation that are extremely pleasant to the reader, joined with a conciseness, which one should think hardly compatible with ease and elegance. F. Simon greatly injures him, when he says, he is rather a paraphrast than a translator; but this is not the only rash assertion, which that Father has made.

Although the Spanish be, perhaps, of all the European tongues, that in which the Scriptures would appear in their greatest dignity; we have, as yet, no Spanish version of them that deserves much notice. Those made by the Jews are barbarous beyond conception*, and that of De Reyna, with all De Valera's improvements, is little more than a servile version from the Latin of Pagninus and Leo Juda.

But to what degree of perfection a Spanish version is capable of being carried, is evident from a translation of the book of Job, made, near two hundred years ago, by F. Luis de Leon.† I know

---

* The only compleat Spanish version of the Hebrew Bible, made by Jews, is that published at Ferrara in 1553; of which the Pentateuch had before been printed at Constantinople, in rabbinical Hebrew characters. From these, the Pentateuch and Aptharoth of Manasseh-ben-Israel, differ but very little. They are useful only as glossaries.

† Luis de Leon was an Augustinian friar, and interpreter of the Scripture in the University of Salamanca. He published, in his own life time, or rather his friends published without his knowledge, an excellent Spanish translation of the Song of Solomon; for which he suffered five years imprisonment, in the dark and inaccessible dungeons of the Inquisition. But those miserable times are happily over; and his Job, which had been long known in manuscript, was printed at Madrid, with all necessary privileges in 1779; together with his learned commentary, and another poetical version, which in many places rivals the sublimity of the original. There is a tolerable Spanish translation of Pindar by the same author.

not if there be, in any language, a verſion that, to the ſtricteſt fidelity, joins ſo much elegance, preciſion and perſpicuity.

I can ſay very little of the tranſlations that have been made into other European dialects; becauſe I am not in the leaſt acquainted with the languages in which they are written. But I am informed by thoſe who are, that they differ not much from our Engliſh verſion; which to ſome of them ſerved as a model. They are all ſtrictly Maſoretical; except that which was made, ſome years ago, into Manks; in the forming of which, I have been told by one of the tranſlators *, attention was paid to the various lections of manuſcripts and other ſources of emendation.

As Lewis has given a detailed, though confuſed, hiſtory of Engliſh Bibles, down to the year 1730; I ſhall only make a few remarks on the principal verſions; and add a catalogue of ſuch whole, or partial tranſlations, as have ſince been attempted.

The firſt compleat edition of an Engliſh verſion of the whole Bible, from the originals, is that of Tyndal's and Coverdale's together †. It was printed abroad in 1537, and known by the name of Matthew's Bible. The violent oppoſition, it had met with at home, ſeems to have ariſen more from the injurious reflections, contained in the prologues and notes, on the then eſtabliſhed religion, than from any capital defects in the verſion itſelf. It was

---

* The reverend Mr. Kelly of Windſor.
† From Geneſis to the end of Chronicles, and the book of Jonah, are by Tyndal; the reſt of the Old Teſtament by Coverdale. The whole New Teſtament is Tyndal's.

far from being a perfect tranflation, it is true; but it was the firft of the kind; and few firft tranflations will, I think, be found preferable to it. It is, aftonifhing how little obfolete the language of it is, even at this day; and, in point of perfpicuity and noble fimplicity, propriety of idiom and purity of ftile, no Englifh verfion has yet furpaffed it. The criticifms of thofe who wrote againft it (we are forry to find Sir Thomas More among them) are generally too fevere, often captious and fometimes evidently unjuft. Of terms nearly fynonymous, Tyndal may have poffibly chofen thofe that were moft favourable to his own religious notions; and, when his original admitted a double fignification, preferred that which feemed the leaft favourable to the tenets he had renounced. This was, doubtlefs, a partiality which every tranflator ought carefully to avoid; but how few tranflators have always been fufficiently on their guard againft its influence.

It was an idle affectation in Tyndal to tranflate *overfeer*, *elder*, *congregation*, inftead of *bifhop*, *prieft*, *church*; as the latter, already become familiar Englifh words, are, in reality, of the fame import with thofe he fubftituted in their place; and there is no more diverfity between the terms, (to ufe an expreffion of Coverdale) than between *four-pence* and *a groat*. It was unfair, and perhaps infidious, in him, to put *image* for *idol*, *ordinance* for *tradition*, *fecret* for *myftery* or *facrament:* but thefe, and fuch like offenfive terms, might have been eafily corrected; nor was it, for that, either neceſſary or expedient to commit the whole work to the flames; which ſerved only to enhance its value, and gave it a greater currency. Burning ſuſpicious books is the readieſt way to multiply them; as perſecuting for religion is the ſureſt mean of propagating it.

Cranmer's *great* Bible, and all the other Bibles that were publiſhed during the reigns of Henry VIII. and Edward VI. are only ſo many improved copies of Tyndal's and Coverdale's tranſlation. In ſome of them the additions that are found in the Greek or in the Latin Vulgate, though not in the preſent original, were judiciouſly inſerted; either in a ſmaller character, or with ſome diſtinguiſhing mark. Tyndal's prologues and notes were alſo generally omitted; and ſome of the moſt exceptionable words altered. The editions reviſed by Taverner recede the fartheſt from their prototype, and are, therefore, the worſt.

In Mary's days, the Engliſh refugees at Geneva ſet about making a new tranſlation, the model of which ſeems to have been the French one of Olivetan, lately reviſed by Calvin and Beza. Hence, and becauſe it was accompanied with marginal notes of the laſt mentioned author, it is known by the name of Beza's Bible. It became the favorite verſion of the puritan party, and went through a great many editions, during the reigns of Elizabeth and James; ſome of which are poſterior even to the laſt reviſion of the Bible. But as the quarter it came from, and the perſons who were concerned in it, made it obnoxious to the Epifcopalians, it was never received as a public ſtandard. King James, in the famous conference at Hampton Court, pronounced it to be the worſt of all Engliſh tranſlations; yet his own tranſlators borrowed more plentifully from it, than from any other; and, to ſay the truth, as a mere Maſoretic verſion, it has conſiderable merit.

In 1586 was publiſhed Parker's, or the Biſhops Bible, which was appointed to be read in churches, as Cranmer's had been before. The greateſt objection made to this tranſlation was, that it deviated too much from the original, in favour of the Greek and Latin verſions. This, we apprehend, would not, at preſent, be accounted a great defect; for the deviations from the original are rarely unwarranted; or, rather, they are only deviations from corrupted copies, or rabbinical comments. But, at that time, the idea had begun to prevail, that the Maſoretic text was inviolably to be adhered to; and this was, probably, the chief cauſe, why the Biſhops Bible was ſo little prized, and ſo ſoon ſuperſeded *.

For, on King James's acceſſion to the throne of England, a new tranſlation was immediately projected, and finiſhed in the ſpace of three or four years; although it was not publiſhed till 1611, when, *by his Majeſty's ſpecial command*, it was appointed to be read in

---

* This tranſlation having become extremely rare, a new edition of it was announced by Hogg in the year 1778: but this edition is a mere counterfeit; being an exact tranſcript of the Geneva Bible.

churches; and has continued, ever since, to be the public authorized version.

The means and the method employed to produce this translation, promised something extremely satisfactory; and great expectations were formed from the united abilities of so many learned men, selected for the purpose, and excited to emulation by the encouragement of a munificent Prince, who had declared himself the patron of the work. Accordingly, the highest eulogiums have been made on it, both by our own writers and by foreigners*; and, indeed, if accuracy, fidelity and the strictest attention to the letter of the text, be supposed to constitute the qualities of an excellent version, this of all versions must, in general, be accounted the most excellent. Every sentence, every word, every syllable, every letter and point seem to have been weighed with the nicest exactitude, and expressed, either in the text or margin, with the greatest precision. Pagninus himself is hardly more literal, and it was well remarked by Robertson, above a hundred years ago, that it may serve for a lexicon of the Hebrew language, as well as for a translation.

It is, however, confessedly not without its faults. Beside those, that are common to it with every version of that age, arising from

---

* F. Simon's *Critique* of this version is little to be regarded. He owns he had no other way of judging of it, but from some scraps translated into Latin or French. It was thus the younger Racine criticized Milton; and thus that Voltaire, from whom better might have been expected (as he had a tolerable knowledge of the English) criticized a writer he was not able to imitate.

faulty originals and Maforetic prepoffeflions, its own intrinfic and peculiar blemifhes appear to be the following.

First, from a fuperstitious attention to render the Hebrew and Greek into literal Englifh, its authors adopted modes of expreffion, which are abhorrent from the Englifh idiom; and, perhaps, from that of all other modern tongues. Our ears, indeed, are now accuftomed to this phrafeology; and the language is become familiar to us, by being the language of the national religion: but a proof that many of thofe expreffions are neither natural nor analogous, is, that they have never yet been able to force their way into common ufage, even in converfation; and he, who fhould employ them, would be fuppofed to jeer at Scripture, or to affect the language of fanaticifm. In fhort, what Selden faid of it is strictly true. "It is rather tranflated into Englifh words, than into Englifh phrafe." From the fame caufe, it is, in many places, obfcure and ambiguous, where a fmall variation in the arrangement of the words, would have made it clear and unequivocal.

Secondly, there is a manifeft want of uniformity in the mode of tranflating *. This was, indeed, unavoidable. The different parts of the Bible were affigned to fo many different perfons, or at leaft

* Dr. Myles Smith, who wrote the preface, feems to have been fenfible of this, when he apologizes, in a certain manner, for a want of "Identity of phrazing." This difference is obfervable, not only in the different portions of Scripture affigned to the different claffes; but often in the fame portion, not feldom in the fame book, and fometimes even in the fame chapter, and fame verfe.

to so many different *Quorums*; and although the whole was ultimately committed to the revisal of six persons, assembled for the purpose, it does not appear, that they made any great change in its first texture. When we consider, that they were only nine months about this revision, we cannot well look for a rigorous examination of the fidelity of the version; much less, for a reduction of its stile to the same colour and complexion *. The books called *Apocrypha* are, in general, I think, better translated than the rest of the Bible; for which one reason may be, that the translators of them were not cramped by the fetters of the Masora.

Thirdly, King James's translators mistook the true meaning of a great many words and sentences by depending too much on modern lexicons, and by paying too little attention to the ancient versions. Many of those mistranslations have been noted and rectified by different commentators, but many still remain unnoticed, and seem to cry for amendment.

Fourthly, in compliance with a novel opinion, that not a word nor particle should be in a vernacular version, that has not another word and particle, exactly corresponding with it, in the Hebrew; and, at the same time, to prevent an obscurity, which would be the necessary consequence of that mode of translating; perhaps, also, to obviate the reproaches of want of fidelity, that had been thrown

---

* It was again revised by Bishop Bilson and Dr. Smith; but what they did, or how long they were employed in this revisal, I have not been able to learn.

out againſt the Biſhops Bible, both by the Catholics and the Puritans; they encumbered their verſion with a load of uſeleſs Italics; often without the leaſt neceſſity, and almoſt always to the detriment of the text. In fact, either the words in Italics are virtually implied in the Hebrew, or they are not. In the former caſe they are a real part of the text, and ſhould be printed in the ſame character: in the latter, they are generally ill aſſorted and clumſy ekes, that may well be ſpared; and which often disfigure the narration under pretence of connecting it *.

Fifthly, King James's tranſlators, like all the tranſlators of their day, were too much guided by theological ſyſtem; and ſeem, on ſome occaſions, to have allowed their religious prejudices to have gotten the better of their judgment. To point out examples, would be an invidious taſk: but it is extremely proper that every tranſlator ſhould have them conſtantly in view, as ſo many cautionary mementos to himſelf.

In fine, through the conſtant fluctuation and progreſs of living languages, there are many words and phraſes, in the vulgar verſion, now become obſolete; a ſpecimen of which may be ſeen in Pilkington's judicious *Remarks*, publiſhed at Cambridge in 1759 †. The

* Since writing the above, I am happy to find that the late Archbiſhop Secker was of the ſame opinion. In his valuable manuſcript notes on the Bible, to which, through the liberality of his preſent worthy ſucceſſor, I have had the moſt free and convenient acceſs; he has daſhed over many thouſands of *Italics*, in the copy of the Engliſh Bible he uſed; and, hardly ever without ſome improvement to the paſſage.

† There is in the Critical Review (vol. xviii. page 101) a liſt of words and phraſes, which

construction, too, is frequently less grammatical, than the present state of our language seems to require; and the arrangement of words and sentences is often such as produces obscurity or ambiguity.

Literal as James's translation is, it did not appear so to Gell, Canne and Ainsworth. The two first projected, and the last partly executed a new version, which was published in a folio volume in 1639*. It was formed, like Cajetan's Latin version, on this absurd principle, that the Scripture cannot be translated too literally; that every word and particle, nay the very arrangement of words and particles are full of mystery, and ought to be preserved with the greatest attention. We are astonished to find in a book written by a man of learning this strange position: " The Holy Spirit " of God often intends a mystery, and so leaves the letter seem- " ingly absurd: such seeming absurdities are left for the honour of " God's Spirit, which clears the difficulties and sets all right †.

But what shall we say of those, who, at a much more enlightened period, have adopted the same servile plan? In the year 1773, was

the authors deemed obsolete or improper; some of which, however, are still used by good writers. As for the long catalogue of words in Purver's appendix, there are at least two thirds of them not only not obsolete, but often more proper than those he would substitute in their place. Indeed, we ought not easily to reject a term, because it is not, perhaps, of the first fashion; especially if it be expressive, euphonic, and sufficiently removed from vulgarity. The nomenclature of our language is not yet so very copious, as to need to be diminished.

* It contains only the Pentateuch, the Psalms and the Song of Solomon. They had been separately published before.

† Dr. Gell's preface to an Essay toward the amendment of the last English translation of the Bible; printed at London in the year 1569.

published a new verſion of the Pentateuch, Joſhua, Judges, and the four books of Kings. It was a poſthumous work of Julius Bate, and is ſaid, in the editor's preface, to have been the reſult of " more " than thirty years indefatigable application to the ſtudy of the " Hebrew ſcriptures." He was undoubtedly well verſed in the Hebrew language, though he ſeems to have paid too little regard to the kindred dialects*: but his learning was deeply imbued with enthuſiaſm; and, on running from one ridiculous ſyſtem, he eagerly embraced another. He deſpiſed the rabbinical but admired the Hutchinſonian *Cabbala!* It muſt, however, be confeſſed that he has tranſlated many particular words and ſentences with great propriety; and his diviſions are frequently more natural than thoſe of the Maſoretes.

In the year 1764, Anthony Purver publiſhed his *New and literal tranſlation of all the books of the Old and New Teſtament, with notes critical and explanatory*. This is ſaid to have been the work of thirty years; and, indeed, it carries on the very face of it undeniable proofs of much reading and infinite labour. After all it is but a rude, incondite and unſhapely pyle; without order, ſymmetry or taſte. It has not even that ſingle indifferent quality which the Critical Reviewers too indulgently allow it to poſſeſs; that of exhibiting a faithful copy of the Maſoretic text; which, I aver, is much more accurately repreſented by the common tranſlation. I

---

* See preface to his Hebrew dictionary.

have paſſed this judgment on the honeſt, but not too modeſt Quaker the more freely, becauſe he himſelf is a moſt deſperate critic who ſpares no one, and dares his competitors to enter the liſts with him. The beſt we can ſay of him, is what Ovid ſays of Phaeton. He attempted what was above his forces, and bravely failed in the attempt—*magnis tamen excidit auſis.* Bad as this verſion is, a tranſlator muſt not think it beneath his notice: it may occaſionally be uſeful to him. He will very often ſee by it, what he is to ſhun; and ſometimes what he may imitate. In a field over-run with cockle, he may, now and then, find an ear of good wheat.

Beſide thoſe general tranſlations, we have ſmaller portions of Holy writ, tranſlated by different hands, ſince the beginning of this century, which it may not be here improper to mention.

A tranſlation of the book of Geneſis, by John Lookup, Eſq. was publiſhed in the year 1740, and dedicated to the Archbiſhop of Canterbury. He ſeems to have ſtudied, with attention, the genius of the original; and, in ſome places, has well expreſſed its meaning: but there is a ſtrange ſingularity in his choice of terms, that often excites ſurpriſe, and ſometimes riſibility.

A new verſion of the three firſt chapters of Geneſis with marginal illuſtrations and critical notes, was given by Abraham Dawſon in 1763; and ſoon after a verſion of the fourth and fifth chapters. Why the Critical Reviewers ſhould think this eſſay the work of a Deiſt, I cannot well conceive. The author is certainly a learned man, and a judicious critic; and we wish he had proceeded in the same career.

Mr. Green of Cambridge published in 1762, his new translation of the Psalms, and in 1781 the poetical parts of the Old Testament: in both which works he has displayed much learning, judgment and taste. We have only to regret that he paid so much deference to the Harian system of Hebrew metre.

Still a model was wanting that should claim every suffrage, and merit universal applause. Need I inform my intelligent reader that such a model at length appeared in the year 1779; when Bishop Lowth favoured the public with his new translation of Isaiah? never did sacred criticism appear with greater dignity than in this invaluable work. Never were the gentleman, the scholar, the grammarian and the theologue more happily united.

So rare an example, set by such a character, could not fail to be copied. Mr. Benjamin Blayney, Rector of Polshott in Wilts, has lately published a translation of Jeremiah, on the same plan; and with great success. I trust he is now employed in some other similar work.

On the same plan Bishop Newcome is labouring on the Minor Prophets; and great expectations are justly formed, from his well known abilities and acumen *.

* Bishop Newcome's translation has appeared; a most learned and valuable work, of which I am happy to have it in my power to avail myself, and from which, I foresee, I shall derive

PROSPECTUS.

Mr. Hopkins, Vicar of Bolney, has given a corrected edition of the vulgar verfion of the book of Exodus; in which he has judicioufly inferted the Samaritan and Septuagint fupplements; when he had reafon to think them genuine. His notes are fhort but generally appofite. May neither " age nor infirmity" prevent him from " profecuting fuch ufeful ftudies *."

We have feveral Englifh tranflations of the Song of Solomon; fome in verfe and fome in profe; and moft of them have confiderable merit. We have, likewife, poetical verfions of Job, the Pfalms, and other detached parts of Scripture; which may be occafionally ufeful to a profe-tranflator: and there are a number of particular paffages, throughout the whole Bible, well rendered and explained, in various critical Commentaries, Effays, Lectures and Sermons; of which a general collection would be of great utility.

Of the New Teftament, befide the verfion, already mentioned, of 1729; we have, fince that, three compleat new tranflations by

---

great advantages. I am only forry that I fhould happen to differ from his Lordfhip about fome of his RULES of tranflating; or rather about fome of the more remote corrollaries he deduces from them: while, at the fame time his great judgment and tafte, and his eftablifhed character as a writer, make me hefitate and doubt about the propriety of fome of my own. I fhall confider both at more leifure and with new attention; and weigh his Lordfhip's reafons with all poffible care and impartiality. In one rule, at leaft, we are perfectly agreed: "The " critical fenfe of paffages fhould be confidered, and not the opinions of any denomination of " Chriftians. The tranflators fhould be philologifts, not controverfialifts."

* See his preface, p. xv.

Wynne, Worsley and Harwood; two of St. Matthew by Scott and Wakefield; and we soon expect, from the pen of Dr. Campbell, a capital work on the four Gospels. But of all these I shall have occasion to speak, more at large, in proper time and place.

A society lately formed for *promoting the knowledge of the Scriptures* have already published some *numbers of Commentaries and Essays*; in which, among other things, they propose to give " an accurate translation of the passage to be explained, with proper divisions into paragraphs and sentences, and pointed with the utmost correctness." We applaud the plan, and heartily wish them success: may we take the liberty to beg of them, to beware of system *.

From the above review of the principal versions made by Protestants, it will, I presume, appear, that their chief and peculiar imperfection is owing to the translators having followed too implicitly the Masoretic text, and paid too little regard to the ancient versions. Let us next see what are the special defects of the translations, that have been made by Catholics.

The number of these, indeed, is comparatively small; an idea having long prevailed, that the Scripture should not be translated into vulgar tongues. It is hard to reconcile this idea with any principle of reason, religion, or sound policy; and we must ascribe

---

* The numbers of this work, which are published occasionally, are sold by Johnson, in St. Paul's church-yard.

it, with some other absurdities, to the ignorance and prejudices of a barbarous age. The first positive decree on this subject was formed, I believe, in a diocesan synod at Thoulouse, in the year 1229; and is not the only exceptionable canon devised by that assembly. In the brighter days of Christianity it was not so. The works of Chrysostome, Basil, Ambrose, Jerom, Austin, are full of the most pressing exhortations to read the Scripture; and the reasons that have, in latter times, been urged against that practice by Mallet and other such writers * deserve not a serious answer. The prohibition was so far from answering the end proposed by it; that it had a quite contrary effect. The separatists from the church of Rome have used no weapon with more success against her, than this one, that was intentionally, but indiscreetly, forged for her particular defence.

It is remarkable, that this doctrine has chiefly obtained in those countries, where the *Inquisition* has been established. In France and Germany a different system has at all times, more or less, prevailed, in spite of the endeavours of some pragmatic zealots to introduce a less liberal discipline. Not to mention a number of manuscript versions, that were in use before the invention of typography; there are, at least, twelve printed editions of a French Bible prior to that of Olivetan, and several German ones before Luther's. Nor was the prohibitory doctrine always countenanced in Italy. We meet

* See a book entitled *Collectio auctorum vulgares versiones damnantium*. Paris 1661.

with thirteen editions of De Malermi's verſion, in the ſpace of leſs than half a century; and all anterior to the aera of the Reformation. From the diſpoſition of the preſent intelligent Pontiff, and from his expreſs declaration, That the Scriptures " are ſources to which all " ought to have free acceſs, in order to draw from them, both a " ſound doctrine and a pure morality," * we have reaſon to expect, that Italian Bibles will ſoon be as common on the other, as French Bibles are on this ſide of the Alps.

Another general prejudice among the Catholics was, that they muſt tranſlate from the Latin Vulgate. This, indeed, was at one time neceſſary: for there were few or none capable of tranſlating from the originals: but why the ſame practice was continued, after the revival of Greek and Hebrew learning, is harder to account for; though the following probable cauſes may be aſſigned.

One, perhaps, was, that they might not be thought to imitate the new reformers; who affected to cry up the originals, in proportion as they cried down the Vulgate. Oppoſition, we know, begets oppoſition. I have read a book written by a Neapolitan Jeſuit, in which he gravely returns thanks to Heaven, that he was ignorant of Greek and Hebrew; for that the knowledge of theſe tongues, was a ſure ſign of hereſy.

---

* *Optimè ſentis, ſi Chriſti fideles ad lectionem divinarum literarum magnopere excitandos exiſtimes. Illi enim ſunt fontes uberrimi, qui cuique patere debent, ad hauriendam et morum et doctrinae ſanctitatem.* From the Pope's letter to Abbate Martini in 1778.

But another more specious, though not more solid reason, for translating from the Latin, was derived from the Council of Trent's having declared it to be an authentic version. This, as I have already said, was by many construed into an absolute and exclusive authenticity; which gave the Vulgate a preference to the Originals themselves. It is plain, however, from the very tenor of the decree, that nothing could be farther from the meaning of the Council: and it has been always allowed by the most learned of the Catholic party, that the Vulgate received no other additional authority from the Synod's declaration, but that of being appointed the sole public Latin version. The Synod did not, could not, give it the smallest degree of intrinsic value which it had not before: for if it was not, before, an authentic version, there had been no authentic version in the Latin church for a thousand years.

The decree of the Council, then, did nothing more than what has been done in most Protestant countries: it established one particular Latin version, as a public standard; to be used in the church-office and in the schools of divinity: and surely of all Latin versions, then extant, the Vulgate, in every respect, deserved the preference. But never did it enter into the minds of that or any other council to ordain, that any version, however excellent, should supplant the originals; or that no other translation should be made from them.

The only plausible reason that can be offered for translating from the Latin, rather than from the originals is, that, the Vulgate having been once adopted as the public Latin verſion, uniformity ſeemed to require that all vernacular verſions ſhould be confonant thereto. But if this motive had unluckily influenced St. Jerom, we ſhould at this day have no Vulgate: for, from the ſame principle, he would have been obliged to tranſlate from the Greek; which had been much more generally received, as a public ſtandard, than ever the Latin was.

It is well known, that there are many paſſages in the Vulgate badly rendered. It is alſo allowed that other faults have crept into it, ſince the days of its author; many of which were not corrected, even by the laſt reviſors: are we to tranſlate theſe faults, and retain thoſe renderings, for the ſake of uniformity? When the Vulgate and the originals agree, which is generally the caſe, a tranſlation, made from the latter, will neceſſarily be confonant with the former; and, at the ſame time, vouch for its fidelity. Where the originals are manifeſtly, or probably, corrupted, whilſt the Vulgate manifeſtly, or probably, reads right; ſtill a good tranſlation will agree with the Vulgate: but is it in the leaſt reaſonable that, where the Vulgate is manifeſtly, or probably, erroneous, the tranſlation ſhould be erroneous too? He muſt be a ſturdy *Vulgatiſt* indeed, who maintains ſo ridiculous a poſition.

The very idea of tranſlating from a tranſlation is a ſtrange idea. We have an excellent French verſion of Plutarch, by Amyot: but would any Engliſhman ſit down to tranſlate Plutarch through the medium of Amyot's verſion? Or could we bear a tranſlation of Q. Curtius, even from the admired verſion of Vaugelas? In the very firſt transfuſion, from one idiom to another, ſome part of the author muſt neceſſarily evaporate: how much more muſt he loſe, on a ſecond or third operation *?

But moſt Catholic tranſlators have not only tranſlated from the Vulgate, but made their verſions more ſervilely literal than was neceſſary, even if they had tranſlated immediately from the originals. This is the more aſtoniſhing, becauſe the Vulgate is a free and liberal verſion; and, as far as Jerom is concerned, not altogether inelegant: whereas the tranſlations that have been made from it, if we except one or two, are ſtiff and barbarous beyond conception. Hence they are often unintelligible †. It would be, moreover, eaſy to ſhew that the greateſt part of thoſe, who have tranſlated from the Vulgate, have very often miſtranſlated it, from not underſtanding or not attending to the originals. The words of the Vulgate are Latin words, it is true; but they have ſometimes ſo uncommon acceptations, and are ſo peculiarly phrazed, that it requires a thorough acquaintance with the Oriental ſtile and knowledge of

---

* Some parts of the Vulgate are tranſlations, from tranſlations.

† " A cloſe tranſlation made at ſecond hand from a free one muſt carry with it a ſtrong " tincture of the medium through which it has paſſed; at the ſame time that it has no chance of " recovering any thing that may have been loſt of the native and genuine colour of the firſt " compoſition." See a ſenſible letter to the Critical Reviewers, vol. xxix. page 78.

PROSPECTUS.

the Oriental tongues, to comprehend their meaning; particularly in the poetical books.

It is evident, I think, from what has been said, that a translator, who works on the originals, can derive but little help from versions made from the Vulgate: and therefore I will not detain the reader with a long enumeration of them.

I have seen but four French translations made from the Latin: that of Louvain, that of Benoit, that of Corbin, and that of Saçi. The first two are little more than the Geneva version accommodated to the Vulgate: the third is beneath criticism: the last is an elegant, secondary, version; and has, with very little variation, been a text-book to all the French commentators for a century past. It appears, however, to be too much a paraphrase; and seldom retains the simplicity and dignity, even of the Vulgate version*.

Until the year 1750, the German Catholics had no tolerable version of the Bible. That of Dietenberg is a bad transcript, or rather miserable interpolation, of Luther's; and Ulenberg's is disgustingly literal and obscure. But, at the forementioned period, a new translation was published by the Benedictines of Ettenheim-Munster, under the direction of F. Cartier, which is, I think, the best translation from the Vulgate, that has yet been made. The reason

---

* Saçy's version was revised and republished by F. Carrieres, with short notes inserted in the text, in Italics; which give it a still more rambling, and often even a ludicrous air.

is obvious: the authors had recourse to the originals, in all dubious cases; and did not strictly adhere to the letter of their text *.

The Flemings have two tolerable versions, the one by De Witt, and the other by Vander-Schuren: but the French language has, for some time past, been so much cultivated by them, that Saçi's Bible is almost as frequently to be met with in the French Netherlands as in France itself.

There are two or three old Italian translations made from the Vulgate †; or adapted to it, from Pagninus's Latin version: but they have not been reprinted for many years back; and have, in reality, little to recommend them. I have not seen Martini's recent version, but I am informed it is very elegant.

In Spain there is not, I believe, at this day a single edited version of the whole Bible. That, which was printed in 1516, was so totally destroyed, that hardly a copy of it is to be found. Some particular books have been lately published; and it is not to be doubted but the rest will soon follow. The torch of learning is but newly lighted up in that ingenious nation: but, if we are not

---

* *Notandum quod illi viris eruditis non satis probentur qui versionem Vulgatae nostrae de verbo ad verbum adornandam esse antumant. Nam praeterquam quod inde sacri textus obscuritas minime tollatur, alienum insuper sensum, spectato verborum tenore, saepius elici manifestum est.* Praefat in Biblia Latino-Germanica. Constantiae, 1763.

† That of De Malermi, first published in the year 1471; that of Marmochini in 1538, and, perhaps, another whose author is not known. See Le Long.

greatly miftaken, it will foon break forth into a blaze of uncommon fplendor *.

Our Saxon anceftors had vernacular verfions of the Scripture as early as the reign of Alfred, who is, himfelf, faid to have been one of the tranflators. Some parts of Aelfric's verfion of the Old Teftament were publifhed by Thwaites in 1698. And we have two different editions of a Saxon New Teftament. All thefe were made from the Vulgate. Hampole, Wiclif and Perry tranflated alfo from the Latin; though, in fome of their verfions, they noted the differences of the Hebrew and Greek, from St. Jerom, Bede and De Lyra †.

From the days of Wiclif there was no verfion made from the Vulgate until the year 1582; when the Englifh Catholics, who had, in the beginning of Queen Elizabeth's reign, taken refuge in Flanders, and were now removed to Reims on account of the war, publifhed a tranflation of the New Teftament only, in one quarto volume. The publication of the Old did not take place till after their return to Douay in 1609. Hence the whole verfion, which

* I am juft now informed by a gentleman, lately arrived from Spain, that a new Spanifh verfion of the whole Scriptures is actually preparing for the prefs; and that, in the mean time, De Valeras' tranflation is permitted to be read; the copies of which are fought with avidity and bought up at any price, at Paris, Amfterdam and other places they can be found in.

† It is a pity the various manufcripts of Wiclif's tranflation, as well as the more ancient Saxon ones, are not carefully collated and publifhed. We fhould, by their means, fee the ftate of the Vulgate at different periods, and be able to trace with more certainty the progrefs of our language.

is in three volumes, is known by the name of the Douay Bible. It is a literal and barbarous tranflation from the Vulgate, before its laft revifion; and accompanied with acrimonious and injurious annotations. Their refidence in a foreign country, and what they deemed a cruel exile from their own, had corrupted the tranflator's language, and foured their tempers; and it was, unhappily, the common cuftom of thofe lamentable times, to feafon every religious controverfy with gall and vinegar. We do not find that Withers, Fulke and Cartwright, who drew their quills againft the Douay annotators, were a bit more courteous in their retorts.

The late moft pious Dr. Chaloner revifed the Douay verfion, on the Clementine edition of the Vulgate; greatly curtailed the annotations; and corrected the ftile, chiefly from King James's tranflation. There are two editions of this revifion; one in the year 1750, and the other in 1764; both in five volumes, fmall octavo. I am told another edition is preparing by the gentlemen of the Englifh college at Douay; and propofals for republifhing it at Dublin, in one quarto volume, are now handed about in London.

Mr. Caryl, a gentleman who had followed the fortune of King James II. publifhed, at St. German's, a new verfion of the Pfalms in 1700; in which, taking Bellarmine for his guide, he has often expreffed the meaning of the Vulgate, much better than the Douay tranflators.

In 1719 Dr. Cornelius Nary publifhed his New Teftament at

Dublin, in one volume octavo; and Dr. Witham's appeared in 1730, in two volumes octavo. There are many good renderings in both thefe verfions.

Mr. W. Webfter, curate of St. Dunftan's in the weft, tranflated the New Teftament from the Vulgate, through the medium of F. Simon's French verfion, and publifhed it at London, in two volumes in quarto, in 1730.

I have in my poffeffion a manufcript New Teftament prepared for the prefs, by the late Mr. Robert Gordon of the Scotch college at Paris; in which fome confiderable miftranflations of all the preceding verfions are noted and rectified *.

But although the Catholics, in general, have made their vernacular verfions of the Bible from the Vulgate; they have not done fo, without exception. Two of the forementioned Italian tranflations, are profeffedly made from the originals. In France, befides Codurc's verfion of Job, Proverbs, Ecclefiafticus and the Song of Solomon, we find a tranflation of the Pfalms by Rodolphe le Maitre; another by Ifaac le Maitre, and another by Dupin; all made from the Hebrew in the laft century; not to mention two compleat manufcript verfions of the whole Bible; one by Dom. Loubineau, a Benedictine monk; and the other by F. Feraud of the Oratory *.

---

* I owe this verfion to Mr. Marmaduke, an ingenious but not very fortunate bookfeller in London; who has alfo favoured me with his own curious manufcript remarks on the Douay Bible, and on Dr. Chaloner's revifion of it.

† See Le Long. append. ad Biblioth. facram.

PROSPECTUS.

In the year 1737 a new verſion of the Pſalms was publiſhed by Dom. Maur d'Antine; and in 1739 appeared Le Gros's firſt edition of *The Holy Bible tranſlated from the original texts, with the various readings of the Vulgate,* &c. printed on a very ſmall type, and in one thick octavo volume. It was republiſhed, with the author's laſt corrections, at Cologne, in 1753, in ſix volumes in twelves. In this tranſlation the additions of the Vulgate are inſerted in the ſame characters with the text; but within crotchets. What is added from other ancient verſions is alſo within crotchets, but in Italics; and the ſupplements, deemed neceſſary to correct or illuſtrate the text, are in Italics, without crotchets.

About the middle of this century, a ſchool of Capuchins was formed at Paris, under the direction of Abbé de Villefroi, for the laudable purpoſe of elucidating the original Scriptures. The Popes Benedict XIV. and Clement XIII. were ſo well pleaſed with the deſign, that they both teſtified their approbation by ſpecial briefs; and the latter honoured the little ſociety with the title of *Clementine*. Beſides an elegant tranſlation of the Pſalms and ſome other books of the Old Teſtament, they have already publiſhed a great many volumes of *Principes diſcutés*, in which there is much ingenuity and conſiderable erudition: but a ſtrong tincture of rabbiniſm imbibed from their maſter, and a violent attachment to a ſpecious but deluſive and dangerous ſyſtem of interpretation, have often led them aſide from the right road, and expoſed them to the too severe though just animadversions of more rational critics *.

We have also a curious and fanciful French version of the Psalms from the Hebrew by Laugeois; in which, although he has certainly taken by far too great liberties with his original, and given novel and arbitrary significations to a number of Hebrew words, there are, nevertheless, many elegant and some uncommonly happy renderings.

The amiable and pious author of *Spectacle de la nature* left behind him a French version of the Psalms and some other small portions of Scripture, which, though professedly made from the Vulgate, has a constant allusion to the Hebrew, and contains some valuable elucidations, especially in the notes.

The last published French version of the Psalms is that of my old condisciple the Abbé Constant, which appeared in 1783, in four volumes in 12mo, and has, I am told, considerable merit.

But a still more important work has been recently announced: a French translation of the whole Bible by the late F. Houbigant; the publication of which is committed to his learned colleague F. Lalande; and will not, we hope, be long delayed.

Having thus seen what helps a translator may derive from former versions, whether in his own or other languages; let us next see what assistance he is likely to receive from interpreters and com-

---

* See *Jugement sur quelques traductions des Pseaumes*, par L'Advocat. *Examen du Pseautier François des Peres Capucins*, par Houbigant.

mentators. Indeed if the light thrown upon the Sacred Writings, were in proportion to the number of those, who have attempted to illustrate them, there would not, at this day, remain the least shade of obscurity: all would be obvious, plain and easy. But of above a myriad of names that appear in the long list of interpreters, nine thousand and nine hundred may, without much detriment, be struck off: and, even of the remaining hundred, there are hardly fifty who are not mere compilators, or servile copyists of one another.

One, who has not read the Fathers, might be apt to imagine that great resources were to be found in their writings. But whoever looks for that, will be miserably disappointed. The Christian writers of the first two centuries were men of great probity; but, generally, of little learning and less taste. They transmitted to posterity the *Depositum*, which they had received from the Apostles and their immediate successors, with great honesty, earnestness and simplicity; and recommended the doctrines they taught more by the sanctity of their lives than by the depth of their erudition. They form so many invaluable links, in the golden chain of universal and Apostolical tradition; but they afford very little help towards clearing up the dark passages of Scripture.

The following ages produced a considerable number of truly learned, and of some very eloquent men; but few of them had the qualifications necessary to form a good Bible-interpreter. There are many excellent homilies on almost every part of Holy Writ, and the just application of an infinite number of particular texts to the most salutary purposes of *instructing, exhorting* and *reproving*, in the volumes of Clement, Cyprian, Cyril, Athanasius, Basil, Ambrose, Augustine, Leo and the Gregories of Nazianzum, Nissa and Rome; and, in these the preacher will always be sure to meet with the best models of true Christian eloquence, joined with the soundest morality. But, if we except Ephrem the Syrian, Origen, Eusebius, Theodoret, Chrysostome, Procopius and Olympiadorus among the Greeks; and Jerom alone among the Latins; I will venture to say, that we shall not easily find, in all the rest, a thousand lines that one would chuse to copy over, in a modern work of Scripture criticism. They generally contented themselves with quoting such copies of the Greek or Latin translations as they had at hand; or, perhaps, often with quoting such parts of them as they could recollect from memory; without ever comparing, or being indeed able to compare them with the originals: and when they could not find a plausible literal explanation of the text thus quoted, they had recourse to figure and allegory *.

* This disposition to allegorize, which has more or less prevailed in every age, ought also to be numbered amongst the causes of imperfect translations: in as much as it evidently determined translators to adopt, of two or more probable renderings, that which most favoured their own propensity. The example and authority of Origen served greatly to propagate this pernicious custom; from the contagion of which few of the succeeding Fathers escaped. The works of Ambrose, Augustine and the Roman Gregory are full of such puerile interpretations:

PROSPECTUS.

In the fucceeding degenerate and dark period, the ftudy of the Scripture was much neglected; and more commentaries were made on the Decretals and the Mafter of Sentences, than on Mofes and the Prophets: yet the firft part of this period, which we may call the brazen age of Chriftianity, produced a Bede, an Alcuin and a Rabanus; in whofe commentaries, if we find little original, we have, at leaft, a tolerable felection from prior commentators. But from the end of the ninth, to the beginning of the fifteenth century, Oecomonius, Theophylactus and De Lyra are almoft the only writers on this fubject, whofe works deferve a perufal.

On the revival of letters, a whole legion of gloffarifts, commentators, and paraphrafts arofe; but not many of them added to the former ftock of Scriptural knowledge. The conteft was, who fhould write the largeft volumes, crowd their pages with the greateft number of quotations, and fay the moft ill-natured things of thofe who happened to be of a different opinion. Not only did the Catholic and the Proteftant write commentaries for the purpofe of confuting one another; but the Scripture became a common arfenal, whence the Dominican drew arms againft the Jefuit, the Je-

---

but it is aftonifhing to find the acute and rational Jerom fometimes carried away in the common vortex. Although both the context and the example of the Septuagint fhould have led him to tranflate Gen. xxvi. 17. "in the *valley* of Gerar", yet he prefers "in the *torrent* of Gerar;" for this fine reafon; that Ifaac, after having been raifed to fuch a pitch of greatnefs, could not poffibly have dwelt in a valley. *Neque enim Ifaac, poftquam magnificatus eft, in valle habitare potuit.*

suit against the Dominican, and the Augustinian against both: while, on the other hand, it supplied various weapons to the Lutheran, the Calvinist, the Socinian, the Anabaptist, and every other denomination of pretended Reformers *.

But though scarcely two interpreters agreed in their explanations, one thing was common to them all. Instead of endeavouring to free the text from the adventitious rubbish, that time and blundering transcribers had heaped upon it; they applied their whole art and industry, to convert that rubbish into genuine ore; or, at least, into such mixt metal, as was current in their own communion. If a few candid and impartial men, such as Erasmus, Drusius, Piscator, Vatablus, Mercerus, Cajetan, Grotius, Capellus, &c. had the courage to deviate from the common track, they

* To this we owe yet another cause of the imperfection of modern translations. Not satisfied with establishing their respective tenets, from the supposed meaning of the words; they sometimes ventured to fit the words themselves to the meaning they wished them to have; and waving, as Gill observes, whatever seemed to make against them, they chose such terms as suited best with their own interest, opinions, and prejudices. Many, and I fear too just, mutual reproaches have been made on this head. I make little account of the invectives of such violent and cavilling writers as Frizon, Veron, Martyn, and Ward; or of the angry retaliations of Amana, Cartwright, Withers, James, and Fulke. They often, on both sides, catched at mere shadows, and found designed mistranslations, where there was no mistranslation at all. But still I believe there was more or less ground for reciprocal impeachment; and I have hardly seen a modern version, in which I could not discern some visible marks of party-zeal. The age of polemical scurrility is, or ought to be, now over; and writers of every persuasion will henceforth, we trust, reciprocally assist one another, towards discovering the genuine signification of such texts or terms as admit of ambiguity; without insidiousness or rancour.

were pointed out by all parties as suspicious and dangerous writers; loaded with injuries and maledictions; and sometimes obliged, according to the testimony of Mariana, to plead their cause in chains. Yet it is chiefly in their works that we are to look for almost all that is truly valuable in the commentaries of the last and preceding centuries.

The young eager Biblical student, who sets out with a resolution of reading whatever has been written on the subject, is frightened, on opening his Le Long, at the formidable host of authors he has to encounter; and, if he be not very steady in his purposes, will be apt to recoil, and decline the enterprise: but let him not despair; I will venture to assure him that the quintessence of all he seeks for is to be found, judiciously collected, and methodically arranged, in Poole's *Synopsis*. Had I always been convinced of this truth, I should have spared myself much fruitless labour, and saved a great deal of lost time: but experience, although a sure, is a slow teacher, *et longo post tempore venit*. Let us husband the moments that yet remain, and endeavour to employ them more usefully.

For, within these last hundred years, things have taken a different turn; and since Capellus pointed out the right way, a number of critics have trodden it with success. By their continued and concurring efforts, the avenues to the sanctuary have been gradually cleared; Masoretic prejudices have been removed; religious animofity has in a great meafure fubfided; and the learned, of all perfuafions, can now bear to walk in the fame path, without juftling one another.

This, like moft other branches of critical learning, begun to flourifh firft in France: thence it found its way into Britain; and is, now, making a rapid progrefs over all Europe, efpecially among the northern nations.

To enumerate all the ufeful books and tracts, that have been written on this fubject, during the forementioned period, would lead me beyond the bounds I have prefcribed to myfelf: but as fome of my readers may, poffibly, wifh to know, by whom this important revolution, in facred literature, has been principally effected; I will juft mention fuch of them, as appear to me to have " laboured more abundantly" than the reft; without meaning to throw any fort of reflection on thofe I may omit.

The works of Capellus, the founder of this *New Academy*, will always claim a particular attention. There are, in all his writings, a clearnefs, a method, and a force that fhould provoke the emulation of every Biblical critic: though few, I fear, will be able to attain them in the fame degree. A new edition of his *Critica Sacra* was publifhed by Vogel at Leipfic in 1777.—Although Bochart be a tedious writer, and although many of his conjectures be extremely dubious, he will feldom be confulted without advantage.— The *Exercitations* and fome other works of Morinus contain a great

number of judicious observations, blended with some paradoxes.—
F. Simon's Critical History is, notwithstanding its few oddities, a
most capital work; and the first, we believe, in which are laid
down just and rational principles, for having a good vernacular
translation of the Bible.—Much just criticism is found dispersed in
the works of Huet, Renaudot, Natalis Alexander, Lamy, Thomas-
sin; the Dissertations of Dupin; the Dissertations, Prefaces, Commentary, and Biblical Dictionary of Calmet; the additional Dissertations and notes of his abridgers; Father Tournemines *Prolegomena*
to his edition of Menochius; Menochius's own Annotations, and
the short but excellent Notes of Emanuel Sa; Pezron's *Antiquité
des tems*, with its defence against Martianay; Martianay's own
pieces on the same subject, and his Preface and Notes to his edition
of St. Jerom; Le Quien's and Souciet's answers to Pezron; Montfaucon's Preface and Notes to Origen's Hexapla, with many scattered remarks in his other works; Houbigant's excellent Prolegomena, Prefaces, and Notes to his Latin version of the Bible; the
work of the Capuchines already mentioned; the Theses and little-
posthumous pieces of L'Advocat*; Constant's Commentary on

---

* First Hebrew professor in the chair of Sorbonne, erected in the year 1751 by the Duke
of Orleans, for the purpose of reviving Oriental learning in the University of Paris, and of ex-
plaining the Hebrew scriptures. No man was more capable of fulfilling this double object
than L'Advocat. He had a penetrating genius, an astonishing memory, a correct judgment,
and an exquisite taste. He was the most universal scholar, the most pleasant teacher, the most
benevolent man and the most moderate theologian I ever knew. Had he lived a little longer

the Psalms, lately published; besides a number of memoires, dissertations, and occasional remarks, in the several journals of Paris, Trevoux, Verdun, Amsterdam, the Hague, and Geneva—all which are deserving of the translator's notice, and will all afford both information and entertainment. Nor are the works of the French Refugees in Holland to be neglected; particularly those of Le Clerc, Le Cene, Spanheim, Basnage, Beausobre, Martin, Chais, Roques, Saurin; most of whom were extremely capable of carrying sacred criticism to a great degree of perfection; had they been less wedded to old prepossessions, and less addicted to theological system.

Among the sacred critics of Italy, the most distinguished are Bartolocci, Cardinal Thomasi, Bianchini, Diodati*, Ugolini, Fabricy, De Magistris, De Rossi, Georgi, Poch, Setaro, Borgia, Ansaldi; many of whom are yet alive; and, I doubt not, heartily labouring in the same vineyard.

In Germany a constellation of writers have lately arisen; who have dispelled more clouds, and cleared up more obscure passages of Scripture, than perhaps the writers of any other nation; our

---

and enjoyed more leisure to accomplish the work he meditated on the Scripture, we should now possess a treasure of great value; but a weakly constitution and too constant an application to his professional duties hurried him away in his 56th year, to the great regret of all who knew him, but of none more than of him who dedicates these lines to his memory.

* Not the same with the translator of the Bible.

own not excepted: although they are not yet arrived at the zenith they fairly promife to attain. At the head of thefe we place the venerable Michaelis, one of the moft learned and judicious modern critics: nor will Biorn-Sthal, Bruns, Fifcher, Hafencamp, Gottfried, Lilienthal, Schulze, Oberlin, Storke, Outhovius, Schoetgenius, Starck, Koppe, Schnurrer, Eichorn, Cramer, Teller, Scheidius, Biel, Knappe, Doederleim, Dathe, Rare, Griefbach, Velthufen, Woide, Maldenhover, Adler, Birch, and other refpectable names, grudge the veteran this honour of precedence; when it is allowed, that every one of themfelves will be a precedent and a model in his turn. There are alfo many pieces in the literary diaries of Leiden, Leipfic, Goetingen, Saxa-Gotha, and Berlin, which the curious and inquifitive indagator will be glad to have difcovered and perufed *.

It may feem an unneceffary affectation to give a catalogue of Englifh writers; who, fince the beginning of this century, have fo largely contributed to emancipate facred criticifm, from the fetters forged by credulity and fuperftition; as the greateft part of my readers may be fuppofed to be, at leaft, as well acquainted with them as myfelf: but, befides, that I cannot, without ingratitude, fupprefs the obligations I lie under to thofe of my country-

---

* The Biblical ftudent will alfo be glad to know that Mr. Maty's new Review contains the earlieft intelligence of foreign publications of every kind; and particulary thofe that relate to facred criticifm.

men who have walked before me in the same career, and smoothed so many places of the rugged path; I observe, with concern, that there are others, who endeavour to throw obstacles in the way; and deter many from entering into it, who might be capable of making uncommon progress.

It is not easy to root out old prejudices even from the minds of the learned. The belief of an immaculate original is not yet universally exploded; and there are who think religion is in danger, if but a single letter or point be altered or expunged. As long as this idea obtains, little more will be done among us towards clearing up the Hebrew writings, than has been done already. Poole, Prideaux, Patrick, Pearce, Hammond, Henry, Whitby, Wells, Wall, Waterland, Clarendon, Clarke, Locke, Sale, Sykes, Stackhouse, Dodd, Watson, and some others of less note have corrected many mistranslations of our present version; and we are greatly indebted to them for their learned labours; but some of them would have laboured much more successfully, if they had raised their superstructures on a better foundation than the supposed integrity of the Masoretic text.

We are not, then, to conclude from the great number of expositors, that therefore the Scriptures are thoroughly expounded. The generality of our commentators, like those of other nations, are either blind followers of some particular theological system; or drudging compilators from different systems. The huge masses

PROSPECTUS.

of indigested matter, that issue yearly from the presses of Fleet-Street and Pater-Noster-Row, are generally better calculated to throw ridicule on the sacred text, than to explain it; and oftener furnish the infidel with specious pretexts, for questioning the truths of religion, than the believer with solid arguments to support them. Expunge from those motly performances the unmeaning mystic jargon, the nauseous cant of enthusiasm, and the trite and tedious maxims of a common-place morality; all that is left behind of any value may be comprest into a nut-shell. Yet these are the guides that direct the people in their Biblical researches. By these the minds of the vulgar are early tinctured with that fanatic zeal, that religious rancour, that horrid intolerantism; the fatal effects of which we so lately experienced; but which could not have happened in a free and liberal nation, like ours, without such potent incitements, as arise from religious prejudices.

To prevent such dangerous consequences, and to rescue the Scriptures from the hands of such empyrics, ought to be the aim and endeavour of every rational theologist. The salutary waters of life should be presented to the people as free of every foreign admixture as possible; and nothing should be presented along with them, that has the least tendency to foment bigotry or create party-rage. Let profound mystics and subtle casuists be, if they will, employed in discovering *allegorical, anagogical*, and *moral* meanings; let professed polemics torment the text, to make it agree with their favourite hypothesis; it is the business of the mere interpreter, much more of the translator, to give the obvious literal sense of his author; with a view to no particular system, and without regard to parties or principles.

Luckily this mode of interpreting has been already adopted by our best writers; and we have only to follow and improve their plan. Whoever has read, with attention, Whiston's Essays on the true text of the Old Testament, Hallett's notes on several texts of Scripture, Mudge and Merrick on the Psalms, Costard's Observations and Dissertations, Pilkington's Remarks, Heath and Peters on Job, Hunt on Proverbs, Desvoeux on Ecclesiastes, Arnold on the Apocrypha; above all Dr. Kennicott's Dissertations on the state of the Hebrew text, and Bishop Lowth's admirable Preface to his translation of Isaiah*, must, we think, be convinced that sacred criticism can never be brought to the perfection of which it is susceptible, but by the method they have pointed out and practised: and his conviction will be still more compleat, if he read the several pieces that have been written on the other side of the question †.

---

* Add to these the Prefaces and Annotations of Blayney and Bishop Newcome, some papers in the Theological Repository, several of Bishop Watson's Theological Tracts, and many excellent occasional remarks in the Monthly and Critical Reviews, and Gentleman's Magazine.

† See Rutherforth's, and the French Abbé's Letters to Kennicott, Robertson's Analysis of the Pentateuch, Baruh's Critica Sacra examined—Durel on the Hebrew text, Horne's View, Purver's Annotations. See also different works of Schmid, Eichorn, Tychsen, Razenberger, &c. &c.

Having thus pretty copiously treated on the principal causes of the imperfection of modern versions, and pointed out what I deemed the surest means of removing them, I will now venture to give my opinion of the distinguishing characters of a good translation; and of the chief qualifications necessary for a translator.

First of all then, a translation of the Bible ought to be faithful; that is, ought to express all the meaning and no more than the meaning of the original. But though this is universally allowed to be the first quality of a good version, it is not easy to determine how it is to be attained: and one of the greatest difficulties I have met with, was to fix upon that precise mode of rendering which should be the best calculated to give a genuine copy of the Scriptures, in intelligible English; without prejudice to the simplicity and dignity of the originals. Two opposite extremes were, I knew, to be equally avoided, a wild paraphrase and a servile version; but in what particular point between them I should rest, or how the happy medium was to be always preserved, were problems, of which, the more I revolved them in my mind, the more hard I experienced it to find a satisfactory solution.

I consulted my learned friends; but they differed so widely in their sentiments, that I was more perplexed than before; and, after all, obliged to rely on my own judgment, such as it is; and to prescribe for myself one uniform route, that seemed the most likely to lead me on, with the least danger, to the intended goal. I entered into it with the greater confidence, becaufe it had been trodden before by Symmachus and Jerom; and recommended by the beft critics of every age, as the fureft way to fucceed.

My tranflation, then, is neither literal nor verbal; but, if I may ufe the term, ftrictly *fentential*; that is, every fentence of the Englifh correfponds as exactly to the Hebrew, as the difference of the two idioms will permit; and although I have not made myfelf fo much a flave to the original, as to adopt its peculiar phrafeology and conftruction, where they greatly differed from our own, I have always kept as clofely to it as was compatible with the ideas I had formed to myfelf of a good tranflation *.

I am not ignorant of the arguments that are urged in favour of a fervilely literal verfion. I have long and ferioufly pondered them, and found them to be light as air. The chief, and indeed the only fpecious one, is that in a free tranflation, there is no fmall danger of fubftituting the tranflator's ideas, in the room of the author's; and confequently of mifleading the reader: but it would be eafy to prove that this danger is greater in literal verfions; and that Pagninus and Montanus are lefs faithful guides than even Caftalio, Michaelis or Wynne. It is indeed abfolutely impoffible to tranflate literally from any language whatever, without being often barba-

---

* *Tranflatio vera eft cujus fenfus a fuo fonte non deviat, fed fententias reddit et eafdem et aequales.* Greg. de Valentia apud Walton.

rous, obscure and equivocal; and this alone is a sufficient reason for translating freely *.

For perspicuity is the second most essential quality of a good translation; nor need we the authority of Horace or Aristotle to establish a proposition so agreeable to common sense. The Jewish, like all other writers, certainly wrote to be understood. The poets and prophets themselves are not obscure on account of their stile; which, though bold and figurative, must have been perfectly intelligible when they wrote; but from our imperfect knowledge of the Hebrew idiom and of the customs and manners of those times. A translator, therefore, who, under the pretext that his originals are

---

* From this the reader must by no means infer that my translation is not a close one. Between *loose* and *liberal* the distance is great; and even of liberal translations there are many various kinds; some of which are little different from what is often, though improperly, called a *literal* version. What I mean is, that perspicuity and the other qualities of a good translation ought never to be sacrificed to a scrupulous adherence to the letter of the original: and, indeed, an English translator will not often have occasion to make such sacrifices. Our language easily moulds itself into the Hebrew form; and it rarely happens that we are under any necessity of having recourse to paraphrase or circumlocution, to express the full meaning of the text. Even when the syntactical arrangement is different, there is a striking equipollence of simplicity, conciseness and energy to be attained; which, perhaps no other modern language can boast of; and which is not found in ours, with regard to any other language, but the Hebrew. With this natural advantage, I flatter myself I shall be able to give a version in nearly as few words as are in the original; and, at any rate, less verbose than even our present vulgar translation. The very few liberties I have taken with the text, to render my version more intelligible, and I flatter myself more energic; and the small deviations I have made from the track of my antecessors, for the sake of a more easy and unembarassed march, shall be noted and examplified, in my General preface.

obscure, affects to give an obscure translation, betrays either his idleness or his ignorance; offers an insult to his reader; and throws an oblique ridicule on the author he pretends to interpret. If the Scriptures are at all to be translated, of which we can have no doubt, they should certainly be made as plain and perspicuous as possible; and not a single ambiguity should be left in them that can be by any means removed. That there are certain mysterious words of the originals, which should not be rendered, may be a pious, but is not a rational notion. The Greek and Hebrew are not, of their own nature, more sacred languages than the Welch or Wallachian: and surely, to a mere English reader, *pass-over* and *praise ye the Lord*, are not less significant and far more edifying sounds than *pasch*, and *hallelujah*.

A third quality of a good version is elegance; but an elegance of a special kind, and of peculiar characteristicks. That an elegant translation of the Bible has a great advantage over a barbarous one, is strongly verified by that of Luther; which would never have been so well received at first, nor continued so long the favourite of the German nation; if it had not, in an eminent degree, possessed the charms of an inchanting stile, and all the graces of a correct and elegant diction. The idle sneer of F. Simon, " that Luther " seemed to have only in view to make the Holy Ghost speak good " German," is in reality a great panegyric; and the aim of Luther ought to be that of every other translator. It is an odd manner of conciliating the taste and fixing the attention of the reader, to tell him, you despise elegancy of composition.

But how is this elegancy to be acquired? Perhaps, it is not entirely to be acquired. It must be, in part, the gift of nature; but the talent may certainly be cultivated and improved; and the observation of the following rules, I apprehend, will be found contributive to that purpose.

In the first place, a translator of taste will be careful to make a just and proper selection of terms. Secondly, he will arrange them in the most natural order. Thirdly, he will reject all meretricious ornaments. Let us illustrate these rules by a few examples.

A proper choice of terms is the first and perhaps the hardest duty of a translator. It is even harder for him, than for an original composer. The latter may accomodate the sentence to his words; but the former is under an absolute necessity of adapting words to sentences. Now as there is, in no language, a perfect *synonymity* of any two terms, it becomes a matter of great difficulty to make always a just distinction. The same Hebrew word, Genesis i. 16. has been rendered *lights, luminaries,* and *illuminations.* The first was the term adopted by our last translators; the second is used by Wells, Stackhouse, and Dodd; and the third by Lookup: but whoever examines the analogical propriety of the three terms, and compares them with the original, will clearly perceive, that *luminaries* is here a more suitable term than *lights,* and *lights* than

PROSPECTUS.

illuminations—To *divide*, to *separate*, and to *distinguish* are words of nearly the same signification; yet I should say, " to *divide* a vic- " tim, a portion, an inheritance, the land, the spoil; to *separate* light " from darkness, waters from waters, the sons of Levi from the " other tribes; to *distinguish* the clean from the unclean, the holy " from the profane, the children of Israel from the Egyptians."

It may, however, happen that a word shall properly enough express the meaning of the original, and yet be inelegant and inadmissible; either, because it is altogether obsolete, or is of low and trite usage, or has some ludicrous idea annexed to it, or, in fine, favours of affectation and pedantry. In all these cases a judicious translator will substitute some more modern, more noble, more decent, and more unaffected term; though, perhaps, it should not be quite so significant and emphatical. *Albeit, fet, hofen, leafing, fith, feeth, fod* were in the days of our forefathers as expressive and congruous words, as those we now use instead of them; yet no translator, who studies elegance, will admit them into his version; much less will he admit such indelicate vulgarisms, as we find in almost every page of Purver's translation; or such quaintness of expression, as is too often chargeable on Le Cene *.

All this, I think, will be readily granted by those who are in the least acquainted with the laws of good writing. But, in the

---

* Both these vices are wonderfully united in a ridiculous and profane version of the New Testament, published with the Greek, in two volumes octavo, in the year 1729.

course of my labours, a doubt has occurred, relative to this subject; which I wish to propose to the consideration of the learned. It has been, I believe, a generally received idea that a translator should prefer words that are originally of the language into which he translates, to words that have been adopted from other languages; and, I confess, I was once strongly prepossessed with this idea. For why, said I, should we have recourse to Greek and Latin, when we can find equivalent terms of good Saxon etymology? I am now convinced I was in the wrong; and that words of a foreign extraction are, not seldom, preferable to those of our own growth. I will give my reasons, and support them by examples.

It will not, I think, be denied, that, of words equally significant, those are the most eligible, which are the least productive of ambiguity, the least liable to receive new and accessary meanings, and the least likely to deviate into triteness and vulgarity *. But to me it appears evident, that words, which we have adopted from other languages, have generally all those qualities in a greater degree than the original terms of our own. They are therefore generally to be preferred. For this reason I should rather say to "*establish*" than "to *set up* a covenant;" "to *regulate*" rather than "to *rule* the day and the night;" *abyss* rather than *deep*; *dismiss* rather than *send away*; *paradise* rather than *garden*; *deludge* rather than *flood*; *conflux* or *assemblage* of waters rather than *gathering together* of waters; *genealogy* rather than *book of the generations*, &c.

* See Michaelis's Dissertation on the influence of opinions on language. Sect. 2.

This rule, however, admits of very many exceptions; and great difcretion, is required in the ufe of it. A word of foreign derivation, though fully naturalized, is often lefs proper than another aboriginal one of the fame fignification. Thus, there is no doubt but that the common verfion of Genefis xi. 8. "The Lord *fcattered* " them;" is preferable to Lookup's: " The Lord *diffipated* them;" although perhaps, *difperfed* would here be better than either. In like manner, I fhould prefer *an iffue of blood* or a *blood iffue* to a *fanguinary flux; after thefe things* to *after thefe tranfactions; nakednefs* to *nudity; power* to *ability; foolifhnefs* to *infatuation*, &c.

It may fometimes even happen, that a word of our own growth and an exotic one of the fame force, are of fuch a nature as to be, refpectively, more proper in one circumftance, and lefs fo in another. Thus, of the terms *drunk* and *inebriated*, I fhould ufe the firft, Job xii. 25. " he maketh them to ftagger, like a *drunk* man:" but the latter Gen. ix. 21. " and he drunk of the wine until he was *inebri-* " *ated;*" for reafons which, I think, will be obvious to every intelligent reader. I would not in the laft inftance tranflate *intoxicated* with Lookup; becaufe intoxication does not properly denote drunkennefs, in as far as it proceeds from excefs in drinking; but from a poifonous quality fuppofed to be in the drink. Again, though *caft out* and *expel* be both good words, yet, if I am not deceived, the laft would be the moft proper word Gen. iii. 24. " So he *expelled* the " man," &c. but, in the mouth of Sarah, Gen. xxi. 10. "*Caft out* that "bond woman" seems to be a more eligible rendering. In short, that term is ever to be preferred, which is the most discriminately expressive of the particular idea, it is meant to convey.

Our last translators paid great attention to this sort of propriety; which gives uncommon beauty and energy to their stile. They generally, indeed, preferred old English terms to recently imported ones *; and, at this day, they may appear to have sometimes carried that preference beyond due bounds: but we should consider, that 174 years are passed since their translation was made; and that many words are now grown familiar to us which were not then at all in use; while many others, that were then of the best usage, have gradually gone into desuetude.

But it is not enough that the words be properly chosen; they must also be properly arranged, we are told that Addison was so scrupulously nice in this particular, that he would often alter a whole paper for the sake of a few misplaced particles. Be this as it may, it is certain that nothing contributes more to elegance than the apposite arrangement of words. " In the beginning God created the heaven and the earth," and " God created the heaven and " the earth in the beginning," are in reality composed of the same terms: but how flat is the last, which is Purver's translation, com-

---

* Sometimes, however, they abandoned this mode of rendering without necessity, and even to the detriment of their version. Ezek. ix. 11. They translate " the man *reported* the matter" instead of " the man brought back word"; though the last be not only a more English, but also a more literal translation.

pared with the first, which is the common one? It is equal, as to the meaning, whether we say with Lookup: " They had served Che-" dorlaomer twelve years, and rebelled in the thirteenth," or with King James's translators, " Twelve years they had served Chedorla-" omer, but in the thirteenth year they rebelled;" yet it will not, we presume, be denied that the latter is by far the most elegant mode of arrangement *.

With regard to meretricious ornaments, the strict mode of rendering which, those who have translated the Scriptures have generally prescribed to themselves, has luckily preserved them from falling into that defect: and this is, perhaps, the strongest argument that can be urged in favour of literal versions. The stile of Pliny, Seneca, or even of Cicero might be clothed, with some degree of seeming propriety, in the English dress of a Stanhope, or Lestrange; but Caesar, Sallust, or Demosthenes would appear strangely metamorphosed in such a garb. Less still does the sacred Scripture admit of this sort of embellishment. The elegance that

* From an improper arrangement of words arises, not only inelegance, but often obscurity and sometimes a misapprehension of the translator's meaning. Instances of this are extremely frequent in Purver. But I shall present the reader with one from the common version. In Ezek. vi. 12. we find these words: " And thou shalt eat it as barley-cakes, and thou shalt " bake it with dung that cometh out of a man, in their sight." By this arrangement it should seem, as if the dung were to come out of the man, in the sight of the people; nor does the comma after man, entirely remove the ambiguity: whereas, transpose the words thus, as they indeed stand in the original: " As barley-cakes thou shalt eat it, and with dung, that cometh " from man, thou shalt bake it in their sight." The sense is plain and obvious, the turn, if I am not mistaken, less prosaical, and yet the translation more literal than before.

suits it is simple and unaffected; not the elegance of a court-lady decked out for a ball or birth-day, but that of rural beauty in her Sunday's apparel, modestly decorated with such flowers as grow in her native meads. The example of Castalio, whose greatest and almost only fault was an affectation to adorn his version with exotic finery, should be a powerful warning to all future translators, to avoid repeating an experiment that proved unsuccefsful even in his hands. Compare his Latin version with that of Houbigant, or Harwood's English New Testament with the vulgar translation, and you will have a striking illustration of what I have here advanced.

A fourth quality of a good translation is as strict a uniformity of stile and manner as is consistent with the other foregoing properties. It should not be close in one place and free in another; sometimes correct, and at other times careless; here, arrayed in the robes of a fashionable taste, and there, only covered with the rags of rusticity; much lefs must it appear a piece of patch work by different hands.

servetur ad imum
Qualis ab incepto procefserit, et sibi conflet.

It does not, however, hence follow, that the same words or even the same phrases should always, and without the least variation, be rendered in the same manner. Those critics, who have required this, have required too much. A compliance with so rigorous a law would often produce a translation not only unintelligible but extremely erroneous. When Lookup, Gen. v. 1. tranflates "This is the *roll* of the hiftories of Adam," he tranflates with fome fort of propriety, becaufe the Hebrew word there fignifies a *narrative*, and narratives were commonly written on *rolls*: but when, Gen. xv. 5. he renders the fame Hebrew term by the fame vernacular one: "Look toward the *roll* of the ftars," he gives to the word *roll* an acceptation of which it is not fufceptible; and, perhaps, imprefles a falfe idea on the mind of his reader. For who would imagine that *roll* here were the fame as *number*; and not rather that it meant *rolling* or *rotation?* not to mention that the original word is in this place a verb, and well rendered in the common verfion, *tell*; ftill better by Bate, *number*.

It is, then, enough that the fame word or phrafe be, in the fame circumftances and in the fame acceptation, tranflated in the fame manner: nor can this be confidered as a hard reftriction on the tranflator; for if he has once hit on a good term or mode of expreffion, why would he feek to change it merely for the fake of variety, at the rifk of ftumbling on a worfe?

Yet this general uniformity in tranflating fhould not preclude a particular attention to that diverfity of ftile which characterifes the different Scripture-writers. This is a fifth quality of a good tranflation, which, however difficult to attain, ought certainly and by all means, to be aimed at. The hiftorical parts of the Bible are not to be rendered in the fame manner, as the poetical; nor thefe, as the sentential. The stile of the book of Job is not the stile of Isaiah, nor the stile of Isaiah that of any other prophet. Every writer, whether sacred or profane, has something peculiar to himself, and it ought to be the endeavour of a translator to retain as much as possible of that peculiarity. He must, as Bishop Lowth finely expresses it, " imitate his features, his air, his gesture, and, as far as " the difference of language will permit, even his voice."

By this time the reader will be sufficiently prepared to draw this inference—That a good translation of the Bible is a most arduous task; and he will, probably, wonder at the resolution, or rashness, of that individual, who ventures singly to undertake it. Nor will his astonishment be lessened by viewing the following sketch of the necessary qualifications of a translator; which with a trembling hand I now venture to delineate.

A translator, then, must in the first place be well acquainted with the language from which, and the language into which he translates; and, for that purpose, must have made a long and serious study of both. It is even hard to say, to which of them he ought to have paid the greatest attention: so nearly balanced are the inconveniences that would ensue from inattention to either.

It is indeed natural enough to suppose that a due knowledge of that language, which we have been accustomed to speak from our infancy, would be much more easily acquired, than that of one, which we are obliged to learn, by the dint of memory, from books.

But that very facility with which we attain our mother-tongue in a certain degree of idiomatical propriety, is a real obstacle to our attaining it in perfection. We are too apt to imagine that he, who readily expresses himself, expresses himself well; and the negligences and even the solecisms of a familiar or provincial stile, will sometimes imperceptibly steal into our most elaborate compositions. There is no colloquial dialect perfectly pure: not that of the capital, not that of the court, not that of the college; and many expressions issue daily from the mouths of our most accurate and polite speakers, that would not bear the test of a severe criticism. A writer must, therefore, be continually on his guard against the obtrusion of a low and vulgar phraseology, and weigh every word and sentence with grammatical skill and logical precision.

On the other hand the difficulty of learning a dead language is evident; especially of such a language as the Hebrew. The compositions in it are few, and incorrectly transmitted to us: the best lexicons are yet very imperfect: the signification of many words is extremely dubious, and their etymology very often equivocal. Hence he, who aspires at but a competent knowledge of it, must frequently have recourse to the other Oriental dialects; the grammar, vocabulary and genius of which he must, consequently, be well acquainted with.

All this is undoubtedly requisite in a translator of the Bible; but it is not all that is requisite. He must, moreover, be converfant in Greek and Roman learning; by means of which, many paſ-ſages of Scripture may be illuſtrated. Poets, philoſophers, hiſtorians, philologiſts, geographers, naturaliſts—all ought to enter into his plan of reading; becauſe from-all he may, occaſionally, derive advantage. Nor ſhould modern travels, voyages and topographical deſcriptions eſcape his notice. In ſhort he muſt be as much as poſſible a univerſal ſcholar; and if he be not ſo capacious a living library, as to retain all he has read; he ſhould, at leaſt, be able to recollect, where to ſeek what he immediately wants.

Yet the moſt profound erudition will not ſecure him ſucceſs, if he be not alſo poſſeſſed of an acute penetration, a nice diſcernment, and a ſure and delicate taſte, formed on the beſt models of antiquity. The moſt of thoſe who have given tranſlations of the Bible were, as Michaelis obſerves * mere ſcholaſtic theologians; who explained the Scriptures according to the ſame dry methodical rules, by which they would have explained the Categories of Ariſtotle. They were even perſwaded that philology had nothing to do with either logic or divinity. *Quanto eris melior grammaticus,* ſaid they, *tanto pejor dialecticus et theologus.* This ridiculous maxim was ſtrongly urged againſt Reuchlin, Valla, Vives, Faber, Eraſmus; and had, before, been urged, with equal ignorance and zeal, againſt St. Jerom. With regard to the interpretation of the Scriptures, the maxim might, perhaps, be inverted: *Quanto melior theologus, tanto*

* Praefat. in notas ad Lowth.

pejor interpres. At any rate, one of the moſt eſſential qualifications of a good tranſlator is to be a good grammarian; without which, all the theology of the Sorbonne will be of little uſe.

From what has been now ſaid, it follows, as a neceſſary corrollary; that a tranſlator of the Bible ſhould have a conſtitution to bear, and an inclination to undergo, aſſiduous and perſeverant labour; a qualification too rarely conjoined with quickneſs of apprehenſion and elegance of taſte. He muſt proſecute his always ſerious, often unengaging ſtudies, with all the warm enthuſiaſm of a poet or painter; and yet with all the patient drudgery of a laborious mechanic. To pore, from morn to eve, on ſuch a number of books, diverſity of tongues and variety of figures, is enough to confuſe the cleareſt intellects; and to deaden the perſpicacity of the mental, as well as of the corporeal eye. If writing the dictionary of a ſingle language be, as Scaliger thought, an adequate puniſhment for parricide; what crime may not be atoned for, by tranſlating the Hebrew ſcriptures?

The laſt, but not leaſt neceſſary, qualification of a tranſlator is an honeſt impartiality. Whether that be abſolutely attainable by any mortal, may be reaſonably queſtioned: but no one will deny, that every poſſible endeavour ſhould be made to attain it. Unwedded to ſyſtems of any kind, literary, phyſical or religious; a tranſlator of the Bible ſhould ſit down to render his author, with the ſame indifference he would ſit down to render Thucydides or

Xenophon. He should try to forget, that he belongs to any particular society of Christians; be extremely jealous of his most rational prepossessions; keep all theological consequences as far out of his sight as possible; and investigate the meaning of his original, by the rules only of a sound and sober criticism; regardless of pleasing or displeasing any party.

Some reader may here be disposed to ask: Are you possessed of all these qualifications? To this not unnatural question I beg leave to give an answer, somewhat similar to that which Cicero gives on a similar occasion; though on a different subject. Having described, with inimitable eloquence, the qualities of an accomplished orator, he modestly declares that he has given, rather an idea of what he conceived to be possible, than of what he ever expected to see. How much greater reason have I to acknowledge that my ideal portraiture of a good translator of the Bible is far beyond the reach of my own abilities.

To be still more explicit and ingenuous; although I have long endeavoured after the qualifications abovementioned, to affirm positively that I have actually acquired them all, or any one of them in an eminent degree, would be an unconscientious and rash assertion. In learning, genius and judgment I know myself to be inferior to many; some few may exceed me in diligence, assiduity and laboriousness; but in candor, impartiality and uprightness of intention I will yield to none.

PROSPECTUS.

It is on thefe more humble and fubordinate qualifications that I principally reſt my hopes of fuccefs; and it is, no doubt, chiefly owing to this part of my known character that my fcheme has been fo generally approved of. For although I belong to a religion that had been long profcribed, and is yet far from being popular in this country; and although my primary intention was to procure a tolerable verſion of the Holy Scriptures for the uſe of the Britiſh Catholics, the flattering and unexpected applauſe I have met with, in every part of the kingdom, from the learned of all communions, makes me hope that my work may be of more general utility than I at firſt imagined; and contribute more or lefs to promote Biblical knowledge over all the land.

To thofe who have encouraged me with their approbation, or aided me by their counfel; or who may, hereafter, be induced to do me the like good offices; I ſhall, in due time and place, make my thankful acknowledgments: but I cannot refrain, at prefent, from mentioning two or three perfons, to whom I have had particular obligations.

The late Dr. Kennicott, on whofe tomb every Biblical ſtudent ought annually to ſtrew the tributary flower, has a peculiar claim to my grateful remembrance. I had hardly made known my deſign, when he anticipated my wiſhes to have his advice and affiſtance towards the execution of it, with a degree of unreferved franknefs and friendſhip, which I had never before experienced in a stranger. Not contented with applauding and encouraging himself, he pushed me forewards from my obscurity to the notice of others: he spoke of me to BARRINGTON; he introduced me to LOWTH. The very short time he lived, after my acquaintance with him, and the few opportunities I had of profiting from his conversation, are distressing reflexions; but still I count it a happiness to have been acquainted with a man, whose labours I have daily occasion to bless, and whose memory I must ever revere.

Another personage, to whom, if my work shall have any merit, the world will stand principally indebted for it, is the Right Honourable Lord PETRE; at whose request it was undertaken, and under whose patronage it is carried on. For although the plan itself is a plan of twenty years standing; and although the author had never any thing so much at heart as its accomplishment; yet his circumstances in life were such, as must have rendered that impossible, without the providential interposition of such a patron. But Lord PETRE is not only the Author's patron; he is in some respects the author. It was his great love for religion, and his extreme desire of seeing Scriptural knowledge more generally promoted among those of his own communion; that suggsted to him the idea of procuring a new translation, before he knew that I had ever entertained a similar idea, and at a time when I had almost despaired of seeing it realized. His Lordship, I trust, will pardon me for inserting, without his knowledge, this public testimony of his piety and munificence; which I could not suppress without violence to my own feelings; and which the public has, in some sort, a right to know.

Bp. Geddes of Edinburgh will, likewise, permit me to say, that his early and warm approbation of my plan made me undertake it with more alacrity and pursue it with greater ardour. His prudent advices and seasonable encouragement have often given a new stimulus to my spirits in the midst of my labours, and sometimes supported me under their almost oppressive load. I trust, from his long uninterrupted friendship, that he will continue the same good offices, until I shall have fairly discharged myself of the heavy burthen; and I foresee I shall yet stand in need of such good offices.

For although I can with pleasure affirm that all those who have hitherto taken the trouble to enquire into the nature of my design, and done me the honour to read my Prospectus while yet in manuscript, have approved of it, without reserve [*]; yet I am not so vain or foolish as to expect that I shall meet with no contradiction in the execution of it. That would be a fate more favourable than befel any of my predecessors in the same career: and I should think my work of little importance indeed, if it totally escaped censure.

[*] I take this occasion to return my warmest thanks to the Bishops of London and Salisbury, Dr. Gosset of London, Principal Robertson of Edinburgh, and Drs. Reid and Findlay of Glasgow; not only for the very favourable manner in which they have been pleased to speak of this Prospectus; but also for some valuable hints of improvement, to which, they will see, I have paid all due regard.

The systematic theologian, and such theologians there are in all communions, can relish no other mode of interpreting Scripture than that which suits with his own partial ideas; and every deviation from these will be by him accounted an unpardonable crime. Bigotry and zealotism will probably roar aloud at my moderation: the sciolist will write to shew that he can write; and envy, malignant envy, has sometimes been seen pursuing objects even as mean as me.

I hope I have a sufficient stock of philosophy and religion to bear even the disappointments that arise from unsuccessfulness in literary pursuits; which I believe to be among the most severe of all disappointments. I only wish not to be judged and condemned without a fair trial. When my translation shall be once published, it will be the Public's as much as mine, and every one will have a right to form what judgment he pleases of it: but until then I earnestly request all Christians in general, and those of my own persuasion in particular, " Not to judge before the time;" nor even then without due examination. My plan is now before them. Let critics point out its defects, and suggest improvements with candor and charity. I will pay attention to their remarks, their admonitions, their strictures; and I promise to

Make use of ev'ry friend and ev'ry foe

towards the rendering of my work less unworthy of the public favour.

For the rest, I am not only well pleased to have it thought, but extremely anxious to have it said and known, that, as a translator,

I am addicted to no particular syſtem; nor guided by any principles but the rules of tranſlating well.

If to future tranſlators I may not be able to exhibit a model of taſte and elegance, I flatter myſelf I ſhall ſet them no common example of religious moderation. It is certainly the intereſt, and ought to be the concern, of both Catholics and Proteſtants, to have their common Code as pure and genuine as poſſible; and their only conteſt, in this reſpect, ſhould be, which ſhall do moſt to clear it from every ſort of corruption. To deſpiſe the labours of another, becauſe he is of a different country or creed, is unworthy of a rational being; and contrary to the practice of the beſt Chriſtian writers of antiquity. Origen was ſo far from depretiating the works of thoſe, who were not of his own communion, that he joined, in the ſame volume, the verſions of Jews and reputed Heretics, with that which the Church uſed: and St. Jerom, profiting of his collection, made no ſcruple to borrow from all of them, as he ſaw occaſion.

It is, indeed, from the united ſtudies of the learned of all communions, that we can ever hope to bring the Scriptures to that degree of purity and perfection, of which they are yet ſuſceptible; and it is with infinite pleaſure we perceive that the learned themſelves begin to be of this ſentiment. The labours of a Houbigant, a Villhoiſon, a Georgi and a Roſſi are as much prized and applauded at London, Leipſick and Goettengen, as thoſe of a Lowth, a Kennicott and a Michaelis are at Paris, Parma and Rome: and if the prefent tafte for Oriental learning continue to be diffufed, we may foon reafonably look for, at leaft, as perfect and impartial editions and tranflations of the Hebrew claffics, as we already have of the Greek and Latin.

I have laid before the Public the nature and end of my undertaking, the difficulties I had to encounter and the means I have ufed to overcome them, the dangers I had to fear and the cautions I have taken to fhun them, the helps I have had, the guides I have chiefly followed, the mode of tranflation I have adopted, the method I have purfued, and the rules I have prefcribed to myfelf in the profecution of my plan: and, now, I look forward, with no fmall anxiety, to that critical day, when the work itfelf muft be fubmitted to the examination of the fame formidable tribunal, from whofe decrees it is in vain for any author to appeal. To be fure of fucceeding, would be arrogance; to defpond, pufillanimity. My hopes are at leaft equal to my fears; and as long as the balance is but equally poized, I will perfevere in holding it.

Should I even fail in the execution of fo vaft a project, there is fome confolation in thinking that I have, in the opinion of good judges, pointed out the right way to fuccefs. My Profpectus, I am told, may ferve as a general chart to younger and more unexperienced ftudents in divinity, who may chufe to embark in the fame perilous voyage. I have delineated with precifion the track which

I judged the safest for them to pursue, indicated the principal landmarks that should direct their course, fixed buoys and beacons wherever I thought there was need, and warned them of such rocks and shallows as they run the greatest risk of making shipwreck upon. Should my own little vessel be, notwithstanding, dashed to pieces, let it be imputed to the unskilfulness of the pilot, not to the impracticability of the passage; and serve only to encrease the wariness and vigilance of the next navigator, without diminishing his intrepidity and spirit of enterprize.

By some, perhaps, it may be expected that I should here give a specimen of my translation and of the form it is to appear in. But, besides that this last is not yet exactly determined, a sketch of the version itself would be but a fallacious criterion, by which to pass a judgment either favourable or unfavourable. I shall be always ready to communicate my ideas and labours to the learned of every denomination, who may do me the honour to interest themselves in my undertaking, and shall pay every sort of due attention to their observations or advice: but I see no reason for gratifying idle curiosity, or malignant censoriousness, by a premature and partial publication. I will, however, subjoin a short notice of the general oeconomy of the work, and so conclude a Prospectus, that by some may, possibly, be deemed already too long.

Although the new version be made from a corrected text of the original, the present printed copies are never departed from, without a special notation. The additions, omissions, transpositions and variations are all distinguished by respective symbols, and supported by corresponding authorities.

The text of the version will be divided into new and more natural sections, the number and contents of which will be printed on the outer margin: but the old division of chapters and verses will, for the reasons abovementioned, be retained, and marked in the inner margin.

The correctional references, various readings, and explanatory notes, will be at the bottom of the page; the critical annotations at the end of the volume.

A new comparative Chronology will accompany every principal transaction, and be expressed in years before Christ, at the top of the page.

With regard to the concordantial references, or parallel passages, with which the margins of our Bibles are crowded; those of them only will be retained that are manifestly real: for the greater number are only distant, and often arbitrary, allusions.

To every Volume, and for the most part to every Book, will be prefixed a particular Preface; in which a compendious critical account will be given of its real or supposed author, its subject, stile and character, and the rank it holds among the Hebrew scriptures in the Jewish and Christian canons.

The whole of the Old Testament will, as far as can be yet conjectured, be comprised in four volumes. The first will contain the Pentateuch and its supplement the Book of Joshua; the second, the rest of the Historical Books in their natural order; the third, the *Hagiographa*; and the fourth, the Prophets. To these it is intended to add a fifth, which, if properly executed, would be an useful introduction to the other four. Beside a general Preface and Indexes, it should contain the discussion of a great number of questions relative to the Hebrew scriptures; their antiquity, authenticity, inspiration, &c. many of which still appear to be susceptible of farther elucidation.

As soon as the First Volume shall be ready for the press, due notice will be given of the time and terms of publication; as likewise at what particular periods the following volumes may be expected.

I have now only to request the learned, into whose hands this Prospectus may come, to favour me with their remarks and strictures on such parts of it as they may think defective or improveable. And if they will, moreover, be so kind as to transmit to me their own observations on any difficult passage of Scripture, I shall consider it as a singular obligation, and make a public acknowledgement of it. Any communications of this kind may be directed to the Author in Maddox Street, or to his Bookseller, R. Faulder, in Bond Street, London.

THE END.

www.ingramcontent.com/pod-product-compliance
Lightning Source LLC
Chambersburg PA
CBHW030311170426
43202CB00009B/954